Radical Dzogchen
The Direct Way to En-Light-enment

L. Ron Gardner

VERNAL POINT
PUBLISHING

Copyright © 2022 by L. Ron Gardner

ALL RIGHTS RESERVED

No part of this book may be reproduced or transmitted in any form or by any means, electronic or mechanical, including photocopying, recording or by any information storage or retrieval system, without written permission from the author and the publisher, except for the inclusion of a brief quotation in a review.

ISBN: 978-0-9836181-5-7

CONTENTS

PREFACE 7

NOTES TO THE READER 9

CHAPTER ONE: DZOGCHEN (THE GREAT PERFECTION) 11
    What is Dzogchen? 11
    The Dharmakaya as the Trikaya 13
    The Practice of Dzogchen (or Atiyoga) 13

CHAPTER TWO: THE TRIKAYA
(THE TRIADIC "STRUCTURE" OF REALITY) 15
    The Trikaya in the Enlightenment Project 15

CHAPTER THREE: RIGPA (PRIMAL PRESENCE) 29
    Rigpa as Radical Gnosis 29

CHAPTER FOUR: TREKCHO
(CUTTING THROUGH SPIRITUAL MATERIALISM) 33
    Trekcho as "Plugged-In" Presence 33

CHAPTER FIVE: TOGAL, PART 1
(CONDUCTING THE CLEAR-LIGHT CONTINUUM) 47
    My Vision of Togal 47

Chapter Six: Togal, Part 2 (The Perversion of Dzogchen) 57

Standard (Canonical) Togal 57
Essential Togal Teachings and Texts (Precious Treasury of the Genuine Meaning, Yeshe Lama, and Naked Seeing) 62
Summary 101

Chapter Seven: Electrical Dzogchen (Plugged-in Presence) 105

The Mechanics of Rigpa in Electrical Terms............. 105
Dzogchen as a Dialectic................................... 106
Ohm's Law and Dzogchen 107
Practice Instructions 110
Questions and Answers 112

Chapter Eight: Christian Dzogchen: The Mystical Eucharist.. 117

Parallels Between Dzogchen and Christian Mysticism 117

Chapter Nine: Daist Dzogchen: Radical Understanding 123

Modern Spiritual Teachings Akin to Dzogchen 123

Chapter Ten: Dzogchen Discussion 133

Open-ended Dzogchen Discussion 133

CHAPTER ELEVEN: DZOGCHEN LITERATURE:
A COGNIZANT OVERVIEW 139
   Recommended Spiritual Texts 139

GLOSSARY 147

SPIRITUAL READING LIST 161

Preface

Dzogchen, the Great Perfection, a.k.a. Atiyoga, has, since its inception, been proclaimed by Tibetan gurus to be the pinnacle of all spiritual paths, the most direct way for a yogi to achieve Buddhahood. Therefore, given my affinity for the highest yoga teachings, it's no surprise that I became smitten with the tradition after I encountered it in the late 1970s through the writings of the esteemed Namkhai Norbu.

In the decades that followed, I read numerous Dzogchen texts by both modern and early Tibetan masters. As a burgeoning expert in mystical traditions who specialized in comparative spirituality, I wanted to understand and be able to explain Dzogchen in relation to other great spiritual traditions. And when, some fifteen years ago, I "cracked the code" of the En-Light-enment project, I knew it was just a matter of time until I applied my demystifying insights to explicating the Great Perfection.

The final "piece" I needed before I could proceed with my Dzogchen exegesis was the availability of texts that describe, in detail, *togal* practices. When these texts, in the past few years, became available to me, I began preliminary work on *Radical Dzogchen*; and after publishing my book *Zen Mind, Thinker's Mind*, I turned my attention to completing this book.

I could, here, spend pages detailing my arguments and insights on Dzogchen, but that would just be repeating the material in the book. Instead, I will simply say that my critique will doubtless be regarded as heretical by many, my deconstruction of canonical Dzogchen teachings will offend many, and my criticism of iconic Dzogchen masters, especially Longchen Rabjam and Namkhai Norbu, will not earn me brownie points in the Dzogchen community. And in response to such reaction, I will simply repeat my mantra: "Dale Carnegie I ain't."

My goal as a mystic-philosopher has always been, and will always be, the radical demystification of spiritual life. And I trust that those who resonate with my goal will appreciate the unique and ground-breaking material in this book.

Notes to the Reader

Except for a handful of terms that have entered the common lexicon (such as yoga, tantra, mantra, guru, and karma), I have generally, but not in all cases, italicized Buddhist and Hindu yogic terms. One of the toughest tasks in writing spiritual books is deciding which terms to capitalize and when. For example, a term such as "Power" might merit capitalization in one context but not another. The calls regarding italicization and capitalization were often subjective, and if I ever do a second edition, I'll doubtless end up changing some of them.

Because this book contains considerable Buddhist and Hindu terminology, I have included an extensive glossary. As with my previous nonfiction books, I have included my Spiritual Reading List, which I've upgraded with new additions.

In reading this book, you'll see that I sometimes capitalize "En-Light-enment" and sometimes don't. In general (though not always), when you see "En-Light-enment" (or "Enlightenment"), I am referring to full or final spiritual Awakening, and when you see "en-Light-enment," I am signifying the process of Awakening via Light-Energy. In borderline cases, where the term could apply to both the process of Awakening and final Awakening, I made a subjective call based on the context in which the term is used.

This book is composed in a question-and-answer format, with the questions and answers derived principally from discussion groups and one-on-one sessions with my students and friends. I have freely edited the questions and answers so as to provide readers with the most enlightening information and instruction. To this end, I have, when pertinent, interjected material from my previous books into the dialogues.

CHAPTER ONE

Dzogchen (The Great Perfection)

What is Dzogchen?

[In this dialogue, the first in a series of Dzogchen discussions between a few of my students and myself, we consider Dzogchen as the primordial State and as the yoga that realizes that State.]

Do you consider Dzogchen to be just a Tibetan tradition, or do you regard it as a universal teaching not limited to the teachings of the Tibetan masters?

The latter. And I'm not the only one with this point of view. Rigpa Wiki (rigpawiki.org), in their entry on Dzogchen, states:

> Dzogchen is both the final and ultimate teaching, and the heart of the teachings of all the Buddhas. Though generally associated with the Nyingma or Ancient School of Tibetan Buddhism founded by Padmasambhava, Dzogchen has been practiced throughout the centuries by masters of all the different schools as their innermost practice. Its origins reach back to before human history, and neither is it limited to Buddhism, nor to Tibet, nor indeed even to this world of ours, as it is recorded that it has existed in thirteen different world systems.

My intent in our series of discussions is to consider Dzogchen from perspectives that critique and transcend those of the Tibetan masters. My goal is to "upgrade" Dzogchen by elaborating it in the context of the Great Traditions, meaning the foremost non-Tibetan spiritual traditions. Moreover, I believe that my own Electrical Spiritual Paradigm (ESP), which I'll elaborate in our discussions, also serves to further the understanding of Dzogchen as primordial and Divine yoga.

What is this primordial state and the yoga that realizes it?

Dzogchen, the "Great Perfection," is the yoga that aims at awakening one to, and continuing one in, the primordial "state" of Being. But truly speaking, this "state" of Being is not a state (meaning a temporary condition), but the non-state, or "State," of unconditioned, uncreated Being-Awareness, termed *Dharmata* in Buddhism. The only yoga that directly realizes (to one degree or another) this transcendental Being-Awareness is the practice of being-awareness (or direct presence) itself. This practice of being-awareness morphs into transcendental Being-Awareness by virtue of the dynamic Light-Energy it engenders. This en-Light-enment, or awakening, process will be elaborated in the course of our discussions.

Dharmata is the *Dharmakaya*, Being-Awareness, or Ultimate Reality, lived and realized as the Condition of all conditions. *Dharmata* is spontaneously realized (to one degree or another) when one is be-ing Being-Awareness, the *Dharmakaya*.

The *Dharmakaya* as the *Trikaya*

You've described Ultimate Reality, or Being-Awareness, as the Dharmakaya, *but in Dzogchen it is often referred to as the* Trikaya, *which consists not only of the* Dharmakaya, *but also the* Sambhogakaya *and the* Nirmanakaya.

Truly speaking, there is only the *Dharmakaya*, but it can best be understood when viewed three-dimensionally as three distinct Dimensions or Bodies. Hence, the *Trikaya*, which is akin to the Shaivist Trinity (*Siva, Shakti, Jiva*) and the Christian Trinity (Father, Holy Spirit, Son), is emphasized in Dzogchen, which, in contrast to most other schools of Buddhism, is a trinitarian Dharma.

We'll consider the *Trikaya* in depth in our discussions, but for now, I'll summarize it thus: The *Dharmakaya* is Being-Consciousness, or timeless Awareness, or universal Mind. When the *Dharmakaya* radiates and "moves" as dynamic Spirit-Power, or Light-Energy, it functions as the *Sambhogakaya*; and when it is realized immanently as Buddha, or Buddha-nature, it is called the *Nirmanakaya*.

The Practice of Dzogchen (or Atiyoga)

Can you describe the practice of Dzogchen?

The term Atiyoga is synonymous (and used interchangeably) with Dzogchen, and means "Utmost yoga." Hence, Dzogchen is the ultimate (or most direct and potent) form of yoga. The fundamental Dzogchen practice is *rigpa*, which means immediate presence, which fosters radical (or gone-to-the root) spiritual understanding. But in order for *rigpa* to "produce," or unveil, the *Dharmakaya* in its fullness, as the *Trikaya*, two things must happen. First, the yogi must cut, or break, through "spiritual materialism" (meaning all that is not Spirit) to get to Spirit, the *Sambhogakaya*; and second, the yogi must commune with (or contemplate and channel) the *Sambhogakaya* (Clear-Light Energy) and then unite with it. The aspect of *rigpa* that focuses on "cutting (or breaking) through spiritual materialism" is termed *trekcho*, and the aspect that emphasizes communion, and then union, with the Spirit, or *Sambhogakaya*, is called *togal*. Upon the attainment of union with the *Sambhogakaya*, the yogi realizes the *Dharmakaya* as his immanent Buddha-nature, the *Nirmanakaya;* and he also realizes the *Dharmakaya* as the *Trikaya*, the three-in-one "structure" of Ultimate Reality.

The Dzogchen books I've read don't describe Dzogchen the way you do.

My descriptions of Dzogchen and definitions of some of its terms differ from those of orthodox Dzogchen. In the course of our discussions, we'll consider these differences as I explain my view of Dzogchen in trans-Tibetan contexts.

CHAPTER TWO

The *Trikaya* (The Triadic "Structure" of Reality)

The *Trikaya* in the Enlightenment Project

What can you say about the Dzogchen Trikaya *and its relevance in the Enlightenment project?*

Plenty. First, I contend that the *Trikaya*, the Buddhist Trinity, has not been properly explained by Dzogchen masters and exponents. And without a proper explanation of the *Trikaya*, the Enlightenment project cannot be properly explicated and elaborated.

Dzogchen masters don't always describe the Trikaya *in the same way. I want to get your take on some of their descriptions, so I can compare your view with theirs. I'll start with Namkhai Norbu, probably the most respected living Dzogchen master.* [Note: Norbu passed not long after our discussion.]

In his book The Cycle of Day and Night, *Norbu describes the Trikaya* [Dharmakaya, Sambhogakaya, Nirmanakaya] *thus:* "The essence of the mind, which is primordially pure, is emptiness and this *is the Dharmakaya. Its Nature is luminous clarity, which is spontaneously self-perfected, and this is the Sambhogakaya. Its Energy is unobstructed and all-pervading and this is the Nirmanakaya.*" But elsewhere in the book, he says, "*The term Nirmanakaya indicates one's material dimension or body, the term Sambhogakaya indicates the subtle dimension of one's energy, and the term Dharmakaya indicates the Dimension of Existence and its inherent Primordial Awareness.*" These descriptions are contradictory and also unclear, because he doesn't elaborate them. What can you say about his descriptions?

You are right. His descriptions of the *Trikaya* are contradictory, unclear, and unelaborated. But this is typical of modern Dzogchen "masters," none of whom, in my opinion, are/were true masters, meaning fully Enlightened beings.

Regarding the *Trikaya*, I contend that it is the same Triple Body as the Hindu Tantric and Christian Trinities. But because Dzogchen is an insular tradition, we don't see Dzogchen "masters" making this connection. I, however, feel moved to do so, because this connection rightly aligns Dzogchen with the other great trinitarian traditions.

Two important points need to be made about the *Trikaya*. First, truly speaking, there is only the *Dharmakaya*: the *Sambhogakaya* and the *Nirmanakaya* are just the *Dharmakaya* in two distinct modes or dimensions of expression. Second, the *Trikaya*, whether as the *Dharmakaya* itself, or in its modes as the *Sambhogakaya* and the *Nirmanakaya*, never enters spacetime. It is unborn and unmanifest, and though it is in, and pervades, the world, it is not of it. Just as Christians err when they bring the Trinity into creation, so do Buddhists with regard to the *Trikaya*.

Now, let's turn to Norbu's descriptions of the three Bodies of the *Trikaya*. In the first description you provided, he identifies emptiness as the *Dharmakaya*. This description is untenable because emptiness is a non-existent with no ontological status. For there to be emptiness, a contingent and derivative quality, there first must be something that is empty. That "something" is Awareness. Awareness is formless, or empty, but it is not formlessness or emptiness. Why does Norbu make this common Dzogchen mistake of identifying emptiness as the *Dharmakaya*? Because he has been infected by what I call the "Madhyamaka virus" (meaning Nagarjuna's illogical emptiness teaching), which is endemic in Dzogchen teachings. Hence, he just ignorantly repeats longstanding Dzogchen dogma.

Norbu, in his first *Trikaya* description, identifies the *Sambhogakaya* as "luminous clarity, which is self-perfected." The *Sambhogakaya* is not "clarity," it is Clear-Light Energy, which bestows "clarity" upon, or to, the yogi. This Clear-Light Energy is not "self-perfected," because the self can do nothing to perfect it. All the imperfect self can do is to converge with this Clear-Light Energy, which "perfects" him by en-Light-ening him.

Norbu then identifies the *Nirmanakaya* as the "Energy [of the mind]" that is "unobstructed and all-pervading." In reality, the Energy he is talking about pertains to Mind, or Consciousness, itself, not to one's mind, which consists of thoughts and feelings, which, in un-En-Light-ened beings, contract, and thereby attenuate, the Energy of Mind, or Consciousness. By not capitalizing mind in his description, he leads us to believe, whether intentionally or not, that he is referring to the individual mind. The Energy (really Clear-Light Energy) that he is describing is, in fact, the *Sambhogakaya*, not the *Nirmanakaya*, which is the embodied Buddha, or Buddha-nature (akin to the Hindu *Atman*/Self and the Christian Christ/Son), through which the *Sambhogakaya* unobstructedly flows and radiates.

Now, let's consider Norbu's second descriptions of the *Trikaya*. Here, he properly describes the *Dharmakaya* as "the Dimension of Existence and its inherent Primordial Awareness." This description mirrors Hinduism's description of Ultimate Reality (*Brahman*) as Being (or Existence)-Consciousness (or Awareness). But unfortunately, few Dzogchen teachers or scholars acknowledge this common Dzogchen and Hindu description of Ultimate Reality.

Norbu errs in his second description of the *Sambhogakaya* when he says it "indicates the subtle dimension of one's energy." The *Sambhogakaya* is the Dimension of the *Dharmakaya* as unborn, transcendental Blessing/Blissing Clear-Light Energy. It is Divine Power, or *Shakti*, not cosmic (or manifest) subtle-body (or *pranic*) energy. Again, the *Trikaya* never enters creation, and none of its Dimensions, or Bodies, can be reduced to individual consciousness, energy, or matter, whether gross or subtle. The full description of Ultimate Reality in Hinduism isn't just

Being-Consciousness (as I described it in the preceding paragraph), but Being-Consciousness-Bliss (*Sat-Cit-Ananda*), which equates to *Dharmakaya-Sambhogakaya*, because *Ananda* implies *Ananda-Shakti*, the same hypostasis as the *Sambhogakaya*, or Bliss Body.

Norbu contradicts his first description of the *Nirmanakaya* in his second when he says that "the Nirmanakaya indicates one's material dimension or body." The *Nirmanakaya* does indicate the material (or emanation) body, but only in the context of its being the manifest container of the immanent *Dharmakaya*, or indwelling Buddha, or Buddha-nature. Hence, the *Nirmanakaya* does not reduce the unmanifest *Dharmakaya* to a manifest hypostasis. Rather, it just describes it in a manifest, anthropological context.

Tenzin Wangyal's descriptions of the Trikaya *in his book* Wonders of the Natural Mind *differ from Norbu's. What can you say about them?*

Wangyal is probably the foremost living expositor of the Bon tradition of Dzogchen, which is similar to Buddhist Dzogchen. The Bon Dzogchen tradition predates that of Buddhist Dzogchen in Tibet, but because the two traditions have intermingled in the same milieu and share Dzogchen commonality, they are much alike. But regarding the *Trikaya*, they differ.

In his book *Wonders of the Natural Mind*, which I have in front of me, Wangyal is all over the place with his descriptions of the *Trikaya* Bodies. Let's first consider his following description: "The Dharmakaya is the emptiness of the natural state of reality; the Sambhogakaya is the clarity of the natural state; the Nirmanakaya is the movement of the energy that arises from the inseparability of emptiness and clarity."

The *Dharmakaya* is not "the emptiness of the natural state of reality"; the *Dharmakaya* is (Ultimate) Reality itself, which is universal, transcendental Awareness. Moreover, the *Dharmakaya*, rather than being empty, is full of, and inseparable from, its own Energy, which is the *Sambhogakaya*. The *Sambhogakaya* is not clarity; it is Clear-Light Energy. "Clarity" describes the state of the yogi who perceives all existents as temporary, non-binding modifications of the Clear Light. The *Nirmanakaya* is not "the energy that arises from the inseparability of emptiness and clarity." Firstly, the *Nirmanakaya* is not energy, but the immanent *Dharmakaya*; secondly, no energy has ever arisen from the "inseparability of clarity and emptiness" because "clarity" and "emptiness" are non-existents, merely secondary, derivative qualities that describe the perceived "conditions" of the primary Existents of Clear-Light Energy (the *Sambhogakaya*) and timeless Awareness (the *Dharmakaya*).

The contemporary Dzogchen texts I've read all use the same terms you've criticized to describe the Trikaya *Bodies. The* Dharmakaya *is always Emptiness, the* Sambhogakaya *is always Clarity, and the* Nirmanakaya *is always Energy*.

It's called "monkey see, monkey do," but Wangyal and Bon get very "creative" beyond these similarities, which is why their *Trikaya* descriptions are worth considering, and criticizing.

Wangyal writes, "In their pure form, the five elements are the cause of the pure Sambhogakaya body or dimension." This is patently absurd. The five elements— space, water, earth, air, and fire—are stepped-down, created derivatives of the uncreated *Sambhogakaya*, which never enters spacetime. The "cause" of the *Sambhogakaya* is the *Dharmakaya*, because the *Sambhogakaya* is nothing but the radiant, or en-Light-ening, "action," or dynamic dimension, of the *Dharmakaya*.

Regarding the *Nirmanakaya*, Wangyal writes, "Whatever concepts, memories, or passions manifest are the Nirmanakaya." Again, Wangyal errs by bringing the *Trikaya* into creation, and in this case, by reducing it to mind-forms. According to Wangyal, "The Nirmanakaya is located in the three channels and the six cakras and, through the potential quality of movement, manifests externally through the five senses." The *Nirmanakaya* is not located in these places, and it does not manifest externally as the five senses. The *Nirmanakaya* is "located" (or felt-realized) in the Heart-center (which is not of the six cakras), and "manifests" (actually radiates externally through a non-*pranic* channel, called *Amrita* (or *Atma*) *Nadi* in Hindu yogic parlance). Although the *Nirmanakaya*'s Energy is, in Norbu's words, "all-pervading and unobstructed," this energy is the *Sambhogakaya* in its emissional form (*Hridaya-Shakti*) rather than in its received form (*Shaktipat*). *Shaktipat* and *Hridaya-Shakti* are Hindu yoga terms that describe *Shakti*, the *Sambhogakaya*, as, respectively, the inflowing (or centripetal) Energy that transforms a yogi into a Buddha (or Realized Self), and the outflowing (or centrifugal) Energy that a fully En-Light-ened yogi ceaselessly radiates.

In Hindu Trika Shaivism, this Heart-Energy, when received, is described as "absorptive and uniting," and when radiated, as "emissional and expansive." This describes the *Sambhogakaya* in its two modes of flow. When a yogi receives this Energy, he is Blessed by it; when a Buddha, a Blessed One, or *Nirmanakaya*, radiates it, he is "compassionately" Blessing all of creation. Only *arya-bodhisattvas* (those who have directly, though impermanently, realized *Tathata*, or Suchness, or Beingness) can receive the *Sambhogakaya* into the Heart-center (*Hridayam*, or *Tathagatagarbha*), and only Buddhas can (unobstructedly) both receive and radiate it.

In my Dzogchen readings, I've only encountered static descriptions of the Sambhogakaya, *such as Clarity, Clear Light, Radiance, or Enjoyment Body. Is it described as Divine Power elsewhere in Buddhism? Or are you the only one who describes it as such?*

I first encountered the *Sambhogakaya* described as Divine Power in *A Brief Glossary of Buddhist Terms*, a publication by the Buddhist Lodge, London. This publication describes the *Sambhogakaya* "as being the vehicle of the Divine Power of the Dharmakaya." This cool little glossary (I have the 1937 Second Edition) also further clarified my understanding of the *Trikaya* with its description of the *Sambhogakaya* as the "condition of the Dharmakaya in Nirvana," as distinct from the *Nirmanakaya*, its "condition in manifestation (Samsara)."

The Dzogchen treatise *The Quintessence of the Dakinis* states, "By attaining the unceasing *Sambhogakaya*, your mind attains mastery of the *Sambhogakaya*." And there are numerous other references in Dzogchen literature to the unceasing nature of the *Sambhogakaya*; but I haven't come across any that unify this description with the concept of the *Sambhogakaya* as Clarity or Clear Light. And I don't recall any Dzogchen descriptions of the *Sambhogakaya* as Divine Power.

How do you reconcile the description of the Sambhogakaya *as static Clear Light with that of dynamic Divine Power?*

My Electrical Spiritual Paradigm (ESP), which I elaborate in my book *Electrical Christianity*, unifies these two descriptions. In short, just as an electrical current generates a corresponding force-field (in this case, a magnetic one), likewise, a spiritual current generates a corresponding force-field (in this case, a radiant, or Clear-Light, one). So, the *Sambhogakaya* can be understood as both a dynamic force-current (Holy Spirit) and its concomitant radiant force-field (Holy Ghost). We'll delve more into this in a later discussion when we consider my Electrical Spiritual Paradigm.

In The Cycle of Night and Day, *Norbu says: "Although unrecognized, the Trikaya is already, from the very beginning, fully manifest as the Essence, Nature, and Energy of the mind. Thus we can say of Dzogchen that the Foundation is the Trikaya, the Path is the Trikaya, and the Fruit is the Trikaya. Dzogchen represents the Phalayana or Fruitional Vehicle, that is to say, the effect is already present as the cause."* What can you say about the Trikaya *in relation to the Base, Path, and Fruit in Dzogchen?*

Norbu's description of the *Trikaya* as the always already Truth of the Base, Path, and Fruit is correct, and it makes clear that for the *Trikaya* to be the timeless Condition of the "mind," it must be unborn and uncreated, and never reduced to cosmic matter or energies. That said, because humans enmeshed in *Maya* (phenomenal reality) are separated from the realization of the *Trikaya* by gross, subtle, and causal sheaths, for them to awaken to the *Trikaya* as the ever-present "Condition of the mind" (uncontracted Consciousness-Energy), they must cut through these sheaths by practicing *trekcho* and *togal*.

Practically speaking, this means uniting one's "mind" (really one's consciousness) with Clear-Light Energy, which "produces," or unveils, the realization of the *Trikaya* as the "already, from the very beginning" Condition of the "mind."

Whether or not one mentally holds the Dzogchen view that the Base, Path, and Fruit are always already the *Trikaya*, the reality for *Maya*-enmeshed humans is that the Path that realizes the Base (timeless, universal Awareness) and "produces," or unveils, the Fruit (Buddhahood, or En-Light-enment) is Di-"vine" yoga—uniting the "vine" of one's consciousness (the contracted *Nirmanakaya*) with the "vine" of Clear-Light Energy (the *Sambhogakaya*). When one's consciousness (the contracted *Nirmanakaya*) is de-contracted by virtue of its union with the *Sambhogakaya*, one becomes an unbound *Nirmanakaya* (or Self, or Christ, or Buddha) whose Essence is the universal *Dharmakaya* and whose Nature is the ceaseless *Sambhogakaya*.

According to Vajra Verses on the Natural State, *a "mind treasure" revealed by the iconic Dzogchen master Jigme Lingpa, "Innate stillness is the dharmakaya, mindfulness arising is the sambhogakaya, and non-duality of stillness and movement is the nirmanakaya." What can you say about this?*

It is loose, faulty descriptions like this that blur the true identity of the *Kayas*. As Ayn Rand put it, "The truth or falsehood of all man's conclusions, inferences, thought and knowledge rests on the truth or falsehood of his definitions."

I'm still not clear on the Nirmanakaya, *because the ways I've seen it described not only differ from your way but from each other.*

The *Nirmanakaya* is typically described in one or other of the following ways: as the unbroken, dynamic Energy of a Buddha; as Compassion or Compassionate Energy; as the form body of a Buddha; and as "responsiveness," meaning the capacity to manifest as anything whatsoever. I contend that the proper definition of *Nirmanakaya* is *Buddha*, which means immanent, or embodied, Mind, or *Dharmakaya*. Hence, I consider *Nirmanakaya* to be a synonym for the Hindu Self (or *Atman*) and the Christian Son (or Christ). In the same vein, I consider *Sambhogakaya* to be a synonym for Hindu *Shakti* and the Christian Holy Spirit; and I equate the *Dharmakaya* with Hindu Siva (who is universal, transcendental Consciousness) and the Christian non-anthropomorphic Father (who is omnipresent Presence).

The Sambhogakaya is also described in different ways, especially as the Light or Bliss Body. But it's also sometimes described as the Reward Body, and I don't know what that means.

There is no end to the faulty descriptions of the *Sambhogakaya* by so-called Dzogchen masters. For example, in *The Supreme Source* (*Kunjed Gyalpo*), Namkhai Norbu defines the *Sambhogakaya* as "the dimension of the richness of qualities." Then he describes it as "the source of the transmission of Tantra [that] corresponds to the aspect of the 'nature' of clarity of the primordial state." If I didn't already know what the *Sambhogakaya* is, I certainly wouldn't get clear on its nature from reading this text.

In truth, the *Sambhogakaya* is the unborn Clear-Light Body (or Dimension), meaning that it is colorless and not a Rainbow Body or any stepped-down subtle body or visionary apparition. It cannot be seen because it is formless and transparent, but it can be felt-experienced as a radiant, ghost-like presence that moves as a Spirit-current. Because it is dynamic, it is better described as the Clear-Light-Energy Body than as the Clear-Light Body. Because it induces the experience of Bliss when (as *Shaktipat*) it descends into the spiritual Heart-center (*Hridayam*, or *Tathagatagarbha*), it can also be described as the Blissing Clear-Light-Energy Body. Because it literally (as poured-down Light-Energy) Blesses yogis who commune with it, it can more fully be described as the Blessing/Blissing Clear-Light-Energy Body. And because, as Blessing Power, or Grace, that is "measured out" and received in degrees commensurate with a yogi's communal (or relational) force, it can also be described as the "Reward Body."

Why is the Trikaya *hardly mentioned in Zen? Is it really a necessary teaching for students of the Way?*

The *Trikayan* (or Trinitarian) model of Reality is hardly a sine qua non for an esoteric spiritual tradition. For instance, Advaita Vedanta, the predominant nondual Hindu tradition, provides no Trinitarian teaching. (In fact, it denies the reality of Divine *Shakti*, discounting it as *Maya-Shakti*.) But from my point of view, spiritual traditions that discount or reject a Trinitarian model of Reality are incapable of adequately describing the "mechanics" of en-Light-enment and the Enlightened Condition itself. Hence, I prefer Dzogchen to Zen and Trika (Kashmir) Shaivism to Advaita Vedanta. But as I've made clear in our discussion, in the case of Dzogchen, its *Trikayan* (or Trinitarian) model is in need of an "upgrade," which I'll continue to provide in the course of our discussions.

CHAPTER THREE

Rigpa
(Primal Presence)

Rigpa as Radical Gnosis

Rigpa *is the prescribed practice in Dzogchen. How would you describe it?*

*R*igpa is the practice of primal presence, which bestows radical (or gone-to-the-root) gnosis (or spiritual knowledge) and whole-body en-Light-enment (or Spirit-current irradiation). It is commonly described as naked or intrinsic awareness, but because one is be-ing (or attempting to be) present *as* this awareness, it is better described as direct and immediate presence.

When a yogi is directly and immediately present, the pressure of his (consciously "plugged-in") presence generates a force that wants to move. When this force is experienced in its "higher" form as descending (or "crashing-down") Energy, then he has awakened to the *Sambhogakaya* in the form of Divine Power, or Clear-Light Energy.

Radical gnosis (or understanding) grows from "standing under" and contemplating the *Sambhogakaya*, the Clear-Light continuum from on high. The yogi understands that his connection to the Clear Light is what en-Light-ens him, and this gnostic understanding prompts him to re-establish (or attempt to re-establish) his connection to it whenever he becomes aware that he has lost it. Permanent union with the Clear Light means that the yogi has acquired a Light Body. It signifies that as an En-Light-ened *Nirmanakaya* (or Buddha), the *Sambhogakaya* and the *Dharmakaya* have become one in, and *as*, him.

Your description of rigpa *sounds just like Hindu yoga, wherein the yogi attempts to unite with universal Spirit, which you equate with Clear-Light Energy, the* Sambhogakaya.

Yes, I equate the two, and I contend that by explaining *rigpa* and Dzogchen in non-Tibetan contexts, including Hindu yoga, I am furthering the understanding and dissemination of what I call the "Esoteric Perennial Philosophy."

Rigpa *is sometimes described as "knowledge of the Ground." How does the yogi acquire this knowledge?*

The Ground is Mind, universal Consciousness or Awareness. It can only be "known" (or yogically realized) in the spiritual Heart-center (termed *Hridayam* in Hindu yoga, and *Tathagatagarbha* in Mahayana Buddhism). The only way to the Heart-center, or "Womb of Buddhahood," is through the descent of Divine Power, the *Sambhogakaya*, which is the same "Body" as Hindu *Shakti* and the Christian Holy Spirit. The descent of this Divine Power, or Light-Energy continuum, "produces" the Four Visions of *Togal*, which are the four progressive states of realization of *Dharmata* (universal Suchness, or Beingness).

CHAPTER THREE: RIGPA

How do trekcho *and* togal *figure into your view of* rigpa?

Trekcho and *togal* are the two fundamental (and complementary) components of *rigpa*. *Trekcho* is the "consciousness" aspect of *rigpa*, wherein the yogi, applying his conscious presence like a diamond-cutter, attempts to cut through spiritual materialism (meaning all that is not Spirit) to get to the "Other Side," which is Spirit, the *Sambhogakaya*. *Togal* is the "conductivity" aspect of *rigpa*, wherein the yogi, who is connected to Spirit, channels, or conducts, its radiant Light-Energy current.

According to Wikipedia, "Rigpa has two aspects, namely kadag *and* lhun grub. Kadag *means 'purity' or specifically 'primordial purity'*. Lhun grub *in Tibetan normally implies automatic, self-caused or spontaneous actions or processes. As quality of* rigpa *it means 'spontaneous presence.'" My question is: How do these two aspects of* rigpa *apply to* trekcho *and* togal?

If you Google the definitions of *trekcho* and *togal*, you will commonly find *trekcho* defined as training in primordial purity and *togal* as directly crossing over to spontaneous presence; hence *trekcho* and *togal*, as the two practices (or sub-practices) of *rigpa*, correlate, respectively, with *kadag* and *lhun grub*, the two "aspects" of *rigpa*.

To sum, although *rigpa* can be understood as the singular enactment or expression of the Great Perfection, in reality, without it being practiced in the forms of both *trekcho* and *togal*, a yogi cannot realize the Great Perfection. In our discussions of *trekcho* and *togal,* we will further consider their roles in *rigpa* and the en-Light-enment project.

CHAPTER FOUR

Trekcho (Cutting through Spiritual Materialism)

Trekcho as "Plugged-In" Presence

You've described trekcho *as "cutting through spiritual materialism to get to Spirit itself." Can you describe this practice in more detail?*

Trekcho, typically defined as "breakthrough," is the implementation of one's consciousness as a "cutting tool" to break through to the "Other Side," which is Spirit, a.k.a. the *Sambhogakaya*. Anything that isn't Spirit, meaning anything that is created, becomes "spiritual materialism" when one's consciousness, through grasping, becomes bound by it. Whether the object (of one's attention) is "gross" (meaning physically present) or "subtle" (meaning a mind form), it becomes spiritual materialism when one's consciousness clings to it rather than connects to and contemplates That which transcends it, meaning Spirit, the *Sambhogakaya*.

The Bible says the same thing when God enjoins us to "put no idols before Me." In other words, any object that "steals" our attention from the Divine becomes a "false idol." *Trekcho* is the spiritual practice of breaking through, or free, of these "false idols" (meaning objects of fascination, distraction, and consolation) to get to the "Other Side," the *Sambhogakaya*.

But I thought that the Dharmakaya, *not the* Sambhogakaya, *is a synonym for God, or the Divine.*

The *Sambhogakaya* is the *Dharmakaya*, the Divine, in its dimension as Clear-Light Energy, or Spirit-Power. It is the *Dharmakaya* in its objectified form as perceivable, receivable Radiance. But in order to realize the *Dharmakaya* in its fullness, as the *Trikaya*, one must unite one's consciousness (or *citta*, or "soul") with the *Sambhogakaya*, which is the same Body, or Hypostasis, as Hindu *Shakti* and the Christian Holy Spirit. Upon the union of one's individual *citta*, or soul, with universal Spirit, the *Sambhogakaya*, the yogi awakens to his *citta* as the *Nirmanakaya* (or Buddha), which, when united with the *Sambhogakaya*, yields realization of the *Trikaya*, the full-dimensional *Dharmakaya* (or universal Mind).

Dzogchen's *Trikaya* En-Light-enment model mirrors Trika (Kashmir) Shaivism's. In Trika Shaivism, the yogi unites his consciousness (*citta*, or contracted *Siva*) with *Shakti*, which de-contracts immanent, contracted *Siva* and yields the realization of *Siva-Shakti*, which equates to *Sat*, the Di-"vine" Being (or *Brahman*), which consists of the "vines" of *Siva* (Consciousness, or Awareness) and *Shakti* (Energy, or Spirit). Just as the union of immanent *Siva* and transcendent *Shakti* "produces" the full realization of the Divine Being, meaning *Sat*, or *Sat-Cit-Ananda*, likewise the union of the *Nirmanakaya* (the immanent *Dharmakaya*) and the *Sambhogakaya* "produces" the full realization of the *Dharmakaya*, meaning the *Trikaya*.

Now, let's return to your original question on getting to Spirit, the *Sambhogakaya*, or *Shakti*. To do this, the yogi must transform his consciousness into a "cutting tool" that penetrates through spiritual materialism. And he does this by assuming and maintaining the *asana,* or "position," of direct, immediate presence. Direct, immediate presence is a synonym for *rigpa*; hence *trekcho* is simply *rigpa* applied as a cutting tool.

I'm not clear on what you mean by "direct, immediate presence." Can you clarify it for me?

I'll explain it a couple of ways. One way to understand it is as awareness-oneness. In other words, the yogi isn't just aware, he's also plugged in to the abstract whole, at-one with existence. Think of it this way: Awareness is like turning a lamp on, but without plugging it in, there is no light or power. *Trekcho* can be likened to consciously plugging in, but until the yogi cuts through his spiritual materialism, a direct connection to the objectified Source, meaning Spirit, isn't possible. Awareness becomes plugged-in presence when one, whole-bodily, lives *as* it in relation to life. Plugging awareness, *as* embodied presence, directly into life transforms it into a penetrating force that cuts through the dross separating one from Spirit. This penetrating force of consciousness, when experienced as a dynamic "pressure," "pushes" the yogi through the dross until he "breaks through" to the "Other Side," meaning Spirit, the *Sambhogakaya*.

A second way to explain presence is to understand it *as* relationship. In other words, plugged-in presence *is* relationship. To be directly, immediately present is to be in, and *as*, relationship. And to be unqualifiedly related is to *be* consciousness. Although relationship implies dualism, when it is direct and unobstructed, it spontaneously morphs into nondual being-consciousness. And when one's consciousness (*as* relationship) is Blessed by the descent of Divine Power into one's Heart-center (located, or felt-experienced, two digits to the right of the center of one's chest), then one's State is that of Divine Being-Consciousness.

In my own meditation practice, I employ the self-enquiry "Avoiding relationship?" whenever I become aware that I have retracted from the *asana*, or "psycho-physical posture," of plugged-in presence. This self (or relational)-enquiry serves to instigate my resumption of the *asana* of relationship.

Trekcho is about generating the consciousness-force to "break through" to the "Other Side." And because relationship, when consciously lived, generates maximal consciousness-force (or pressure), it is the definitive *trekcho* practice.

So, relationship is the epitome of trekcho?

Yes. The *asana* of direct relationship, when enacted, spontaneously organizes one's consciousness into a penetrating force that cuts through spiritual materialism. Hence, in the words of the great spiritual adept Adi Da Samraj (1939-2008), "Relationship is the discipline."

Relationship implies relationship to something. What is one supposed to be in relationship to?

Everything and anything. Relationship can be to the abstract whole, to empty space, or to objects (gross or subtle) arising or abiding within space, including one's body and mind. Ultimately, one cuts through all these and encounters the ultimate Object, Spirit itself. And when one's consciousness unites with Spirit, relationship morphs into nondual Being-Awareness.

Practically speaking, empty space is an ideal object for one's contemplative (or relational) focus, which is why Dzogchen emphasizes it. Basic Dzogchen practice often begins with simple "gazing into space." And once your attentional "gaze" is stabilized, you should then practice being in direct relationship to space.

What's so special about empty space as an object of contemplation?

First, it functions as a mirror that reflects your activity back to you. In the context of relationship to empty space, you can clearly and objectively view your thoughts. Most importantly, you can see and feel them as formations of consciousness that contract the field of open awareness into enclosed states of self-constriction. When you can see and feel this, your response should be to let go of the grasping mind-forms that generate the self-contraction, the "clenched fist of consciousness" that is suffering.

Second, empty space functions as a doorway to Spirit, the *Sambhogakaya*. When empty space begins to "dance," to come alive as "gift waves" of *Shakti*, this Blessing Power, or Clear-Light Energy, literally en-Lightens you, outshining your thought-forms. Conducting and resting in this Light-Energy continuum is the essence of *togal*, which we'll consider in detail in our next discussion [see Chapter Five].

What is empty space?

It is the *Akasha* (Sanskrit *Akasa*), the formless, universal Space element, a.k.a. the ether. The *Akasha*, or ether, is the primal ethereal "substance" that underlies and pervades the cosmos. It is the root element from which the four gross elements (fire, earth, air, and water) derive. Tibetan Buddhists err when they conflate emptiness or empty space with the *Dharmakaya*, which is timeless, spaceless Awareness. Space is a created substance or element, whereas the *Dharmakaya* is uncreated Being-Consciousness.

Interestingly, *Akash*, which is the corresponding word to *Akasha*, means "Sky" in many Indo-Aryan languages; hence, when Dzogchen students are instructed to gaze into the open sky in front of them, this is tantamount to focusing one's attention on the ether.

In Dzogchen, three different ways of thoughts self-liberating themselves are described. What can you say about this?

First off, thoughts don't self-liberate because thoughts aren't bound and in need of liberation. Liberation pertains to the self, meaning the individual or yogi. That said, Dzogchen's three ways of liberating oneself from thoughts are valid and represent a continuum of reduced effort. The first, or most "effortful," of the three ways is that of bare or naked attention, wherein the yogi looks directly at the thoughts, thereby dissolving them. This level has been described as "like a dew drop evaporating in the sun."

The second of the three ways is that of indirectly vanishing thoughts by neither accepting nor rejecting them. This approach, which is akin to J. Krishnamurti's choiceless awareness, involves some effort, because one must practice allowing thoughts to just be and dissolve of their own accord. This level has been described as "like snow melting as it falls into the sea."

The third, or effortless, way, is that of Self-liberation itself. When one is rested in the Self, or Buddha-nature, superfluous thoughts are incinerated in the radiant Intensity of the Clear Light, and functional thoughts are spontaneously un-done as soon as they have done their work. This level has been described as "like a snake unwinding the coils of its own body."

Beyond thoughts, what are the obstructions to uniting with Spirit, the Clear-Light continuum?

Besides the mind (conscious and sub-conscious), the obstacles, or sheaths, of spiritual materialism that one must cut through include the gross, or physical, body, the subtle, or individual *pranic* (etheric), body, and, ultimately, Spirit, or the *Sambhogakaya*, itself, because when it is objectified as a Dimension or Body separate from Being-Consciousness, the *Dharmakaya*, it functions as a sheath that veils the Vision of *Dharmata*, the True Nature of existence.

How is one to cut through these sheaths? Simply by practicing *trekcho*, which means being directly and immediately present to, and through, whatever arises. And when the yogi's consciousness intersects the *Sambhogakaya*, the Holy Spirit, *trekcho* morphs into *togal*—contemplation of the Clear-Light continuum.

Beyond the "monkey," or discursive, mind, Dzogchen texts pay scant attention to the other sheaths of spiritual materialism, which are more deeply considered in the Hindu yoga traditions. Let's now consider the classic five sheaths that, per Vedantic philosophy, veil the Absolute.

The first sheath (*annamaya kosha*) is one's gross, or "meat," body. This physical "vehicle" can be viewed negatively (as a temporarily animated carcass) or positively (as a temple of the Divine). Regardless of how one views the body, it has to be "cut through," or penetrated (and interpenetrated), by the "diamond" of consciousness.

The second sheath (*pranamaya kosha*) is one's vital, or subtle-energetic, body. This sheath is reflected in one's *nadis*, *chakras*, and aura. When a yogi begins to cut through the sheaths, *Kundalini* (coiled "Serpent Power") awakens, and this uncoiling power can be felt as a pressure and movement in both the gross and subtle-energetic bodies. The practice of *pranayama*—consciously focusing on one's breathing cycle—intensifies the pressure and movement of this subtle, or etheric, energy. There can be no en-Light-enment without this cosmic-etheric energy cutting the knots in one's subtle body. But the subtle body should not be confused with the causal body, the true Spirit Body/Energy, which severs the yogi's causal (or Heart)-knot

The third sheath (*manomaya kosha*) is one's "lower" mind, one's mental habit-energies, or psychical proclivities, which generate entanglement with, and bondage to, "gross" phenomena (e.g., money, food, and sex) and "subtle" phenomena (e.g., one's judgments, memories, and emotions). When one's mind (*citta* functioning as *manas*) dwells upon and grasps hold of objects, gross or subtle, then one's consciousness has contracted into the activity called "lower mind." But when one's consciousness (*citta*) begins to function as *Cit* (pure Consciousness itself) rather than as *manas* (mental formations), then one begins to cut through, or transcend, the "spiritual materialism" generated by this sheath.

The fourth sheath (*vijnana kosha*, a.k.a. *buddhi*) is one's "higher" mind, or ascertaining intelligence, which enables one to perceive the self-contracting nature of his mind (*manas*). The "higher mind" not only enables a yogi to recognize the binding nature of his mental activity, it also instigates his transcendence of the mind by informing him to live from the "position" of Consciousness Itself (*Cit*) rather than to be enmeshed in self-entangling mind-forms.

The fifth, and final, sheath (*anandamaya kosha*) is the causal body, which, in and of itself, is not a sheath, but pure Spirit, the Energetic Dimension of the Absolute, a.k.a. the *Sambhogakaya*. But because the yogi cannot transcend subject-Object entanglement with this Light, or Bliss, Body until this Body itself, functioning as Blessing Power, or Grace (*Anugraha-Shakti*), severs his Heart-knot (*Hridaya-granthi*), it is considered a sheath from the viewpoint of the path.

Can you summarize what you've said so far about trekcho *as a cutting tool?*

Trekcho is the "tool" the yogi uses to cut through spiritual materialism to get to Spirit, the "Other Side." When his consciousness assumes the *asana* of relationship (or awareness-oneness), it morphs into a diamond-like cutting tool that penetrates (and interpenetrates) the first four sheaths until it encounters Spirit, Divine Power. Then, in turn, it penetrates, and is penetrated by, Spirit itself, which the yogi receives as *Shaktipat*—downpoured Blessing Power. When this Spirit-Power, or *Shakti*, cuts the yogi's Heart-knot, it permanently unites with his consciousness or "soul" (*citta*), and frees it for all eternity. At this Divine "juncture," spiritual materialism has been forever cut through by the yogi, the "diamond cutter" par excellence.

Trekcho is *rigpa*, direct naked presence, applied to "breaking one through" to the *Sambhogakaya*, the Spirit-current. *Rigpa* as *trekcho*, or "plugged-in" presence, "organizes" one's consciousness into an adamantine intensity that penetrates through the obstructions to the Spirit-current, which one contemplates, conducts, and unites with in *togal*. Plugged-in presence is a synonym for direct, immediate relationship. When relationship, as plugged-in presence, is unobstructed, one's consciousness intersects the *Sambhogakaya*, the radiant Spirit-current, or Clear-Light continuum, and one proceeds, progressively, through the Four Visions of *Togal*.

In Tilopa's *Song of Mahamudra*, Tilopa sings, "The void needs no reliance, Mahamudra rests on naught." Likewise, the void, or empty space, needs no reliance in Dzogchen, but is a recommended object of contemplation because it provides an ideal "backdrop" or "something" to focus one's attention on. This is the case because thoughts tend to dissolve when one "stares into space." And as the *pranically* charged ether, the void serves as a direct portal to Spirit. A recommended adjunct practice is to consciously breathe (or inhale and exhale) the empty space, which, in an "initiated" yogi, suffuses his body with *prana* and intensifies his connection to space and Spirit. A final word on empty space: One can freely gaze into it, but real *trekcho* practice is to be in relationship to, and through, it, to the "Other Side," the *Sambhogakaya*.

The reason the Instruction Series (which consists of *trekcho* and *togal*) developed and then superseded the two previous Dzogchen Series (the Mind Series and the Space Series) was because the en-Light-enment project could not be properly engaged and understood without breaking it into two separate (and complementary) practices. *Rigpa's* two aspects (*kadag* and *lhun grub*) imply two practices, but these practices weren't made explicit until the Instruction Series formalized them as *trekcho* and *togal*.

In A Treasure Trove of Scriptural Transmission: A Commentary on The Precious Treasury of the Basic Space of Phenomena, *Longchen Rabjam writes: "Freedom comes about through the effortful cultivations of the visions of togal… Alternatively, freedom comes about effortlessly through the realization of trekcho." What can you say about this?*

One of Dzogchen's biggest mistakes was its original emphasis on effortlessness, the practice of which is apotheosized by Rabjam in *A Treasure Trove of Scriptural Transmission: A Commentary on The Precious Treasury of the Basic Space of Phenomena*. In this text, Rabjam mentions *togal* only a few times. Instead, he promotes *trekcho*, which he repeatedly describes as an effortless practice (in contrast to *togal*, which involves effort). The truth is, Rabjam has it backwards: True *trekcho*, the practice of presence, involves conscious effort, whereas true *togal*, the practice of conducting the Clear-Light continuum, is quasi-effortless.

Wow! Dissing the great Rabjam like that almost borders on heresy.

You haven't heard the least of my criticisms of Rabjam. Wait until we get to the second part of our two-part *togal* consideration. Then you'll see what I really think of him.

Other descriptions of trekcho also make it sound like a letting go and letting loose practice.

It is, but only secondarily. First and foremost, it's a cutting and penetrating practice. John Myrdhin Reynolds makes this clear in his book *The Golden Letters*, wherein he writes, "In fact, this directly penetrating Awareness represents in itself the unification of view, the meditation, the conduct, and the fruit of the natural Great Perfection."

In order to transform one's awareness into a penetrating "cutting tool," one must be whole-bodily present to what arises. Consciously assuming and maintaining this *asana* of "plugged-in" presence, or relationship, is a discipline that takes some effort. This *asana* of presence generates a force or pressure that wants to move. To allow it to move, or flow, one must let go (or self-empty); hence *trekcho* can be described as a dialectic of presence/absence, wherein presence is the thesis, absence is the antithesis, and power is the synthesis. And when one receives/conducts this power as *Shaktipat*, the descent of Divine Power, then *trekcho* has morphed into *togal*.

We've hardly exhausted the ways to view and describe *trekcho*, and when we turn our attention to non-Tibetan traditions, we'll consider some of them.

CHAPTER FIVE

Togal, Part 1 (Conducting the Clear-Light Continuum)

My Vision of Togal

What can you say about togal? *You seem to reject the way it's presented by Dzogchen masters, both past and present.*

First off, because I'm well-versed on the subject, I speak knowledgeably of *togal* teachings. Beyond the knowledge I've gleaned from general Dzogchen texts, I've studied the two foremost canonical Dzogchen *togal* texts—Longchen Rabjam's *Precious Treasury of the Genuine Meaning* and Jigme Lingpa's *Yeshe Lama*—along with a number of other texts that focus on *togal*, including, but not limited to, Sam van Schaik's *Approaching the Great Perfection: Simultaneous and Gradual Methods of Dzogchen Practice in the Longchen Nyingtig*, Christopher Hatchell's *Naked Seeing: The Great Perfection, the Wheel of Time and Visionary Buddhism in Renaissance Tibet*, and John Myrdhin Reynolds' *The Practice of Dzogchen in the Zhang-Zhung Tradition of Tibet*. Secondly, based on my study of canonical *togal* teachings, I have little regard for them. Just as I consider Nagarjuna to be the great subverter/

perverter of original Buddhism, I likewise consider Longchen Rabjam, through his *Precious Treasury of the Genuine Meaning*, to be the great subverter/perverter of the Great Perfection. For it was Rabjam, through this text (a commentary and elaboration on the *Seventeen Tantras* of the Esoteric Instruction Series), who championed these canonical *togal* teachings, which I reject as true *togal*. And it was Jigme Lingpa, through his *Longchen Nyingtik* corpus of literature (especially *Yeshe Lama*), who promulgated them.

Because the *togal* I teach hardly accords with that of Rabjam, Jigme Lingpa, and the Dzogchen masters who have followed them, I'm going to divide our consideration of the practice into two sessions: this one, which will focus primarily on my version of the practice, and a second one, which will critique standard canonical *togal* teachings.

Common definitions of *togal* include "leap over," "direct crossing," "direct vision of Reality," and "spontaneous presence." "Leap over" and "direct crossing" imply that the yogi bypasses *trekcho* and immediately connects to and contemplates the Clear-Light continuum. "Direct vision of Reality" and "spontaneous presence" describe this connected state. For until the yogi's consciousness converges with the Clear Light, he cannot experience a "direct vision of reality" and enjoy a state of "spontaneous presence."

An advanced yogi can, at times, directly and immediately "leap over" spiritual materialism to Spirit itself, the "Other Side." Once he "leaps over" to the "Other Side," "locks-in" to the Spirit, the *Sambhogakaya*, and begins to channel it, his infused contemplation (which allows him to rest in the Spirit-current) can be described as a state of "spontaneous presence."

But until a yogi is fully Enlightened, there will be times when he cannot practice *togal* (directly connecting to the Clear-Light continuum, or Spirit-current) and must resort to *trekcho* (cutting through spiritual materialism to get to the "Other Side," the Spirit, or *Sambhogakaya*). Viewed from the perspective of Hindu tantra, *trekcho* can be likened to the discipline of *Satsang* (the attempt to achieve at-one-ment with Divine Presence/Power), while *togal* is akin to *Shaktipat* (directly connecting to Divine Presence/Power and receiving its Light-Energy).

Do you consider togal *a separate practice from* trekcho *or just an extension of it?*

It's an inseparable extension of *trekcho*, and Longchen Rabjam agrees. He writes, "People who cling to Thregchod [Trekcho] and Thodgal [Togal] separately and practice accordingly are similar to a blind person examining forms." But Rabjam, who is contradiction-riddled, also disagrees with this assessment, and this is exemplified in *Precious Treasury of the Genuine Meaning*, wherein he enumerates seven ways in which *togal* is superior to *trekcho*.

Prior to the Instruction Series, Dzogchen yogis just practiced *rigpa*, direct immediate presence, which, in its mature, or empowered, stage morphs into Clear-Light conductivity. But in order to explain the differences between the empowered and the pre-empowered stages of *rigpa*, Dzogchen masters divided them into two distinct practices: *togal* and *trekcho*. Just as *Trikaya* metaphysics was developed to more clearly explain distinctions between the essence, nature, and embodiment of the *Dharmakaya*, *rigpa* was likewise divided into *trekcho* and *togal* in order to more descriptively explain its "mechanics."

Isn't your description of togal *dualistic, contrary to the nondual Dzogchen approach?*

Complain to Longchen Rabjam! He describes Dzogchen as "the union of the ultimate sphere and intrinsic awareness," which implies two distinct dimensions of Reality. The fact is, Di-"vine" yoga, which involves the union of the "vine" of consciousness (or awareness) and the "vine" of Spirit (or Clear-Light Energy), is a nondual practice. This is so because intrinsic awareness and Light-Energy are only *apparently* separate. But from the perspective of a *Maya*-enmeshed yogi, who must, literally, cut through the sheaths that prevent his nondual realization of intrinsic awareness and the Clear Light, this separation is an ontic reality.

Can you describe the stages of Enlightenment engendered by the infusion of Light-Energy in togal?

There are "Four Visions" (or four stages) of *togal*, and Dzogchen master Namkhai Norbu describes them thus:

> The first of the Four Visions of Thodgal [Togal] is called the 'Vision of Dharmata' (or 'nature of reality') and the second vision is the further development of the first. The third is the maturation of it, and the fourth is the consummation of existence.

As Norbu's description makes clear, there aren't four separate visions; there is a single "vision" that intensifies or matures until it culminates in the realization, or "Vision," of *Dharmata*, universal Suchness, or Beingness.

I contend that *togal* is simply channeling/contemplating the *Sambhogakaya*, a.k.a. the *Dharmamegha* (or Dharma Cloud) in both Hindu and Buddhist traditions. In Mahayana's Ten Stages (*Bhumis*) of a Bodhisattva's Enlightenment, the final four stages are classified as "pure," and the first six stages as "impure." This is so because the unborn, immaculate Clear Light is "Purity" itself, while disciplines and practices that don't involve Clear-Light Energy are considered "impure."

When the descent of the *Dharmamegha* (or Dharma Cloud) into the spiritual Heart-center (*Tathagatagarbha* in Mahayana, *Hridayam* in Hinduism) is "full-blown," meaning that the Heart-knot has been cut (called the Heart-release by the Buddha), then *Bodhicitta* is attained. *Bodhicitta* means Conscious Light, or En-Light-ened Consciousness, and signifies the permanent union of one's consciousness (*citta*) with Clear-Light Energy, the *Sambhogakaya*, or Dharma Cloud. As such, despite claims to the contrary by parochial Buddhists, this is the same realization as in Hindu yoga, wherein the yogi's individual consciousness permanently unites with universal Spirit, the *Shakti*.

Longchen Rabjam, in *A Treasure Trove of Scriptural Transmission: A Commentary on The Precious Treasury of the Basic Space of Phenomena*, defines *togal* as "resting in the continuum of the radiance of Awareness." This is tantamount to a Christian mystic channeling the Holy Spirit, a Jewish mystic receiving the Supernal Influx, and a Hindu yogi conducting the *Shakti*-current. Again, Dzogchen is not superior to other forms of pure mysticism; it's just "packaged" and "marketed" to convince its followers that it is.

What of the Four Visions? Again, they simply refer to the depth (or intensity and fullness) of the descent of the *Sambhogakaya*. The "Clear" Light is clear, meaning it can't be seen. Rather, it is felt-intuited. "Seeing" the Light is just a figure of speech. Yes, one can see all kinds of things (especially in the dark), including *thigle* (spheres of rainbow light), but this is a manifestation of Clear-Light Energy, and not the unmanifest Clear Light itself. One gets a Light Body (meaning Spirit as an inseparable "consort") when the fourth "Vision" is attained, but any "rainbow" manifestation is superfluous to this attainment.

Namkhai Norbu and other contemporary Dzogchen teachers do not agree with my view of *togal* and the Four Visions. Instead, they shroud the practice of *togal* in secretive mystery, holding it out as the proverbial carrot in front of the "donkey," meaning the naive disciple. Regarding *togal* (*thodgal*), Norbu writes:

> This practice is genuinely secret, and it is not appropriate to give more than the most basic description of it here. This is not the same as an instruction for practice. Thodgal is found only in the Dzogchen teachings.

According to Norbu, (though he doesn't elaborate beyond this), "Through the development of the Four Lights, the Four Visions of Thodgal arise, and working with the inseparability of vision and emptiness one proceeds until the realization of the Body of Light is attained."

My response to Norbu (and Dzogchen teachers who share his view) is: Real *togal* has nothing to do with "secret" teachings involving visions that one gets while gazing at the sun or meditating in dark caves or rooms. It has nothing to do with visual experiences of *thigle* or any lights correlated with the Four Visions. The Four Visions, in fact, are "visions" of the Clear Light, which is invisible and can only be felt-experienced.

To mystics steeped in the Esoteric Perennial Philosophy, the Four Visions in Dzogchen are akin to the Four *Jhanas* in original (or Pali) Buddhism, the seventh to tenth *bhumis* (or stages) of a *bodhisattva's* en-Light-enment in some Yogacara schemas, and the four levels of Grace in Christian mysticism.

In some Yogacara schemas, the seventh to tenth stages of the ten stages of a *bodhisattva's* en-Light-enment are simply the progressive intensification of the descent of the *Dharmamegha* (or Dharma Cloud). The full descent of the *Dharmamegha* (or downpoured *Sambhogakaya*) into the *Tathagatagarbha* (or Sacred Heart-center), yields *Bodhicitta*, or *Tathata* (which is the same Divine Condition as *Dharmata*). Hence, it's likely that the Dzogchen tradition simply adopted the final four stages of a *bodhisattva's* en-Light-enment, and "mystified" it by "packaging" it as "secret *togal* teachings."

With regard to Christianity, I believe that the First Vision correlates with Baptism, the Second with Confirmation, the Third with Sanctifying Grace, and the Fourth with Divine Union/Beatitude. Each of these "Visions" is simply the intensification of the descent of the Holy Spirit, or *Sambhogakaya*, until consummating Divine Union, or Supreme Beingness, is realized. *Dharmata* is a synonym for Suchness, or Beingness, and the union of the "vine" of one's soul (or consciousness) with the "vine" of Spirit, the *Sambhogakaya*, "produces," or unveils, Di-"vine," or Supreme, Beingness, the *Dharmata*. This is coincident with attaining a Light Body, because the *Sambhogakaya* is the Light Body.

In Dzogchen, the Third Vision is said to reveal a full, though not yet permanent, vision of the *Dharmata*. This vision correlates with Sanctifying Grace in Christianity, which signifies the attainment of sanctuary in the Sacred Heart-center (equivalent to the Heart-Essence in Dzogchen). When Grace, the Descent of the Holy Spirit, or *Sambhogakaya*, intersects the contracted *Nirmanakaya* in the Heart-center, and de-contracts it, *Dharmata*, Divine Beingness, stands out as the True Nature of existence.

Can you describe togal *practice in more detail?*

As I see it, there are three variations of *togal* practice: one yin, one yang, and one neutral. The yin practice is that of being an empty container that consciously receives, and is filled, to one degree or another, with the Blessing/Blissing Light-Energy of the downpoured *Sambhogakaya*. The yang practice is that of consciously converging with the *Sambhogakaya*. And the neutral practice is that of resting in the Light-Energy continuum. In a single meditation session, an advanced practitioner can, more than once, cycle between these three variations. Because spiritual contemplation is an art, the yogi, employing "skillful means," must determine which variation(s) of *togal* he should emphasize in a given session.

You said that Longchen Rabjam describes togal *as "resting in the continuum of the radiance of awareness." This accords with your description of "true" togal, so what's your beef with Rabjam's* togal *teachings?*

Over the years, I had read numerous Dzogchen texts, including three tomes of Longchen Rabjam's teachings—*The Practice of Dzogchen*, *The Precious Treasury of the Way of Abiding*, and *A Treasure Trove of Scriptural Transmission: A Commentary on The Precious Treasury of the Basic Space of Phenomena*—and in none of these does Rabjam mention secret *togal* teachings or methods involving visions or visual experiences that one might experience in dark caves or while sun gazing. In fact, *togal* is hardly mentioned in these texts, beyond being summarily described by Rabjam in terms such as "resting in the continuum of the radiance of awareness." So, based on these texts, I wrongly assumed that the subversion/perversion of Dzogchen through *togal* teachings, which I had encountered in bits and pieces in other texts, had been perpetrated by masters who followed after Rabjam. But when I finally read texts that detailed the historical roots of *togal*, I learned that Rabjam himself was the guilty party. And because some of these texts—especially Rabjam's *Precious Treasury of the Genuine Meaning* and Jigme Lingpa's *Yeshe Lama*—detail these *togal* practices, I also learned how reductive, remedial, and antithetical to the spirit of true Dzogchen they are. In our next session on *togal* [see Chapter Six, Togal, Part 2], we'll consider these practices as well as other aspects of these teachings.

CHAPTER SIX

Togal, Part 2 (The Perversion of Dzogchen)

Standard (Canonical) *Togal*

In our first *togal* discussion [Chapter Five, Togal, Part 1], we focused on *togal* as I teach it. In this session, we're going to consider it as it's classically taught, via the canonical texts *Precious Treasury of the Genuine Meaning* by Longchen Rabjam and *Yeshe Lama* by Jigme Lingpa. And we'll also reference other texts that provide enlightening insights and commentary on the subject. Before we begin, are there any questions?

Yes. Namkhai Norbu writes that "Dzogchen is neither Sutra nor Tantra," and John Myrdhin Reynolds [his student and a noted Dzogchen scholar] echoes his statement. Given that togal *is clearly tantra, is there any basis for their view?*

None that I'm aware of. In fact, *togal* philosophy and practices stem from the *Seventeen Tantras*, which Rabjam comments and elaborates on in *Precious Treasury of the Genuine Meaning*. And other writers have no problem identifying Dzogchen and *togal* as tantric. For example, consider the following excerpt from the Introduction to *Yeshe Lama* by Tulku Thondup Rinpoche in the Snow Lion publication, translated by Lama Chonam and Sangye Khandro:

> The *Yeshe Lama* [the core togal teaching of Jigme Lingpa's *Longchen Nyingtig*, which became, and remains, the fundamental canonical togal teaching] encompasses the essence of all the Great Perfection tantras. In Great Perfection, there are three classes of teachings: those of mind, expanse, and upadesha. The division of upadesha has four cycles: outer, inner, esoteric, and innermost esoteric (or heart essence). The teachings given in the *Yeshe Lama,* especially those on togal, are based on the innermost esoteric cycle. They are superior to all the other vehicles.

Tulku Thondup Rinpoche's statement makes it clear that Dzogchen and *togal* are tantric teachings. And in alignment with Longchen Rabjam and Jigme Lingpa, it asserts that *togal* teachings are "superior to all other vehicles." But, in fact, much of these teachings are just a mishmash of rituals and methods that derive from Mahayoga and Anuyoga, tantras that Dzogchen rates as inferior to the Great Perfection, a.k.a. Atiyoga. And when I describe these *togal* practices, it will be evident to serious *rigpa* students that they are remedial tantra, and thus don't qualify as true "Great Perfection" teachings.

Students interested in the genesis of *togal* teachings and the history of their incorporation into the Great Perfection should read Sam van Schaik's scholarly *Approaching the Great Perfection: Simultaneous and Gradual Methods of Dzogchen Practice in the Longchen Nyingtig*. Van Schaik describes the inherent tension between what he terms the "simultaneous" methods of the original Great Perfection and the "gradualist" ones in the *Longchen Nyingtig*. And in contradistinction to claims by Lingpa and others for the superiority of the *togal* vehicle, he identifies these teachings as recycled, lower tantra teachings. He writes:

> It has been said that the *Longchen Nyingtig* marks a critical point in the merging of the Great Perfection with the rituals of mahayoga, the assumption being that from the fourteenth century onward, Great Perfection cycles came to incorporate more and more mahayoga material, and that this becomes especially apparent with the *Longchen Nyingtig*. However, treasure collections much earlier than the *Longchen Nyingtig* can be identified that contain an equal or higher proportion of mahayoga, anuyoga, and general ritual texts than the *Longchen Nyingtig*.

How did Lingpa and other defenders of the gradualist approach (meaning *togal*) justify its incorporation into the Dzogchen corpus? Van Schaik explains:

> For those defending the gradualist approach, there are very few, perhaps in this degenerate age none at all, who are suitable for the simultaneist approach. This is the position that Jigme Lingpa tends toward in his authorial texts in the *Longchen Nyingtig*. As I will show in the following chapters, he attempts to teach a gradualist path without contradicting the voice of the treasure texts, which speak in the language of simultaneism.

Can you go into more detail on the history of togal *and how Rabjam, Lingpa, and others justified its superiority?*

For the full story, get van Schaik's book. Briefly, Rabjam, in the fourteenth century, revitalized the corpus of literature known as the Seminal Heart, a collection of texts called the *Seventeen Tantras*. And in two texts, the *Tegcho Dzo* and the *Tsigzon Dzo* (translated as *Precious Treasure of the Genuine Meaning*), he, per van Schaik, "set down in a coherent and systematic form, the miscellaneous doctrines and practices contained in the Seminal Heart collections." But by the eighteenth century, the Seminal Heart was, in the words of van Schaik, "beginning to look like a number of competing and increasingly divergent practices." Enter Jigme Lingpa, in the eighteenth century, who, through his work (or "treasure cycle") the *Longchen Nyingtig*, which was based on Rabjam's Seminal Heart system, established the Seminal Heart as a normative set of practices within the Nyingmapa tradition (the Tibetan Buddhist school whose hallmark is Dzogchen).

How did Rabjam, Lingpa, and others justify the superiority of the Seminal Heart *togal* teachings? Through lies, bullshit, and exaggerations. Because that is the only way reductive, remedial tantra teachings can be promoted as superior to the true Great Perfection. Until relatively recent English translations of these teachings (such as *Precious Treasury of the Genuine Meaning* and *Yeshe Lama*) became publicly available, these teachings were shrouded in mystery, only accessible through personal tutelage under a Tibetan lama. But with the cat now out of the bag, so to speak, Dzogchen students can now judge these teachings for themselves.

So, in your judgment, Rabjam and Lingpa fail to teach the "gradualist" path of togal without contradicting the "simultaneist" way of the Great Perfection?

Yes. And they not only fail, but end up perverting the Great Perfection in their attempts to reconcile the two paths.

Why would they resort to such bullshit and deception?

A few reasons come to mind. First, they knew that relatively few Great Perfection students could properly practice *rigpa*, so, to sell the tradition, they resorted to seductive visionary practices and marketed them under the guise of the Great Perfection. Because competing traditions also resorted to pushing reductive tantric practices under false claims and pretenses, they felt compelled to do the same. And because the practices were not made public, but only given to students privately under vows of secrecy, they weren't concerned with their "charade" being exposed.

Do you believe that any of these teachings were really termas *["treasure teachings"] buried or hidden by earlier masters and then later recovered?*

No. And I likewise don't buy the mind *terma* claims. For example, I don't take seriously Jigme Lingpa's claim that Longchen Rabjam transmitted blessings and teachings to him that led to the creation of the *Longchen Nyingtig*.

Essential Togal Teachings and Texts (*Precious Treasury of the Genuine Meaning, Yeshe Lama,* and *Naked Seeing*)

If, as a student of Dzogchen, you have any real intelligence and discrimination, upon reading Longchen Rabjam's *Precious Treasury of the Meaning*, translated by Lama Chonam and Sangye Khandre, you will summarily dismiss it as spiritual crappola, as the perversion, rather than the pinnacle, of the Great Perfection. Although the translation itself is awful, the "Dharma" dispensed by Rabjam, through his commentary on the *Seventeen Tantras*, is equally atrocious, as is the quoted material itself. Rabjam, seemingly sans a sapient critical faculty, can find no fault with any of the *Tantras* he comments on. Hence, I can only view him as an unapologetic peddler of practices and philosophy that are counter to both the letter and the spirit of the Great Perfection.

Precious Treasury of the Genuine Meaning is a tome so bursting with balderdash that it would take an equally long tome to properly deconstruct it. But given that I lack the interest to undertake such a herculean task, a brief consideration of the text in the context of our *togal* discussion will have to suffice. And given the overwhelming amount of poppycock permeating the text, it's easy to find sample material to comment on. I'll start my deconstruction by presenting some excerpts from the text, followed by my commentary.

> The aggregates of wanderers are the kayas of the buddhas, primordially so; yet no one is aware of this. These aggregates as buddha [nature] emerge through the development of their syllables present within their energy channels.

First, if no one is aware that the "aggregates of wanderers are the kayas of the buddhas," then how is Rabjam? Second, it is utter nonsense to state that "aggregates as buddha [nature] emerge through the development of their syllables present within their energy channels." Anyone who believes that there are syllables present within the energy channels is delusional. But Rabjam goes even a step further when he combines the syllabic baloney with elemental bunkum to describe the development of the human embryo:

> On the fifth day, the water and earth energies synthesize the embryo as a single entity and cause it to stabilize. By the sixth, fire and wind accelerate maturity and definition. By the seventh day, based on the function of the neutral element of space expanding, the four above elements unify; and within the four subtle channels, the four syllables *kham*, *sum*, *ram*, and *yam* clearly form in association with their corresponding element.

The text's description of the embryo's development continues, and to give you an idea of how poppycock-laden it is, here's its description for the twenty-ninth to the forty-second day:

From the twenty-ninth to the thirty-fifth days, the process of maturity continues; and during that time, fire's energy of dispersing and balancing is activated by anger. Through the force of earth's energies, there is a process of destruction that acts as the cause for revealing various distinctions of karmic deeds. From the thirty-sixth to the forty-second day, the process of wind's forceful gathering and dispersing is generated by hatred.

Here's an excerpt that links green light with *prajna* (wisdom):

Through the green light, the cause for the luminosity of self-emergent prajna occurs, originating from the channel of the wind that emerges at the time of the path.

Green light has nothing whatsoever to do with *prajna*, nor with anything spiritual for that matter. I've read 3,000 + spiritual texts, and I have never encountered a single sage in any tradition other than *togal* who identifies a connection between green light and *prajna*.

Here's an excerpt that ascribes discernment to the winds (*pranic* movements):

The five divisions of the heat-assimilating winds are the wind that discerns pure versus impure that is nondual with the life essence wind that generates warmth nondual with awareness, wind that clarifies things nondual with luminosities, wind that synthesizes the nondual with the bindus, and the elevating wind that is nondual with prajna.

Wind does not, and cannot, discern or clarify anything. And the idea that there is dual wind and nondual wind is farcical. The winds (*vayus* in Hindu yoga) pertain to life processes, and, like all other cosmic phenomena, are neither dual nor nondual, but simply exist.

The writing in this text is awful. Here's a typical example:

> The way of abiding is threefold: the nature is threefold: the nature abides as kayas, the intrinsic nature abides as bindus, and compassion as wisdom luminosity. First, the peaceful kayas abide in the heart; and from the dynamic strength of their radiance, the wrathful deities appear in the skull.

What "nature" is threefold and abides as *kayas*? And how does the "intrinsic nature" differ from the "nature"? The text doesn't say. It is absurd to say that compassion abides as wisdom luminosity or anything else.

The Reverberation of Sound is the root tantra of the *Seventeen Tantras* and the one most quoted by Rabjam in *Precious Treasury of the Genuine Meaning*. Here is a sample of its nonsensical teachings:

> Through the right ear, the karmic winds manifest. Through the left ear, sound is heard as wisdom.

It is ridiculous to say that sound is heard as wisdom, and just as ridiculous to associate this with the left ear. Wisdom is not something that is heard; rather, it is real intelligence or deep insight that humans exercise in relation to inner and outer experiences.

Here's another example from *The Reverberation of Sound*:

> The characteristics of pristine space itself are that it is the dual aspect of self-perfected blueness, a perfect inclusion of upaya and prajna. From the corners [of the eyes], the two kayas are sustained; and all-encompassing phenomena will then increase.

What can one say about such gobbledygook? There is no "self-perfected blueness" because blueness is not a self that can perfect itself. Moreover, space is not a perfect inclusion of *upaya* (skillful means) and *prajna* (wisdom), because space can neither include nor exclude anything. The idea that the two *kayas* (the excerpt doesn't specify which two, but probably means the *Dharmakaya* and the *Rupakaya*) are sustained through the corners of the eyes is utterly inane. A blind yogi can realize the *kayas*, because realization of the *kayas* is sustained through one's conscious awareness, not the corners of one's eyes.

I bought the book, and it is pathetic. You could go on all day and night shredding it.

Right, which is why I'll now move on to describing the *togal* practices, then finish by disclosing the outlandish claims for *siddhis* the text makes. Before I begin, I again want to emphasize that the practices and claims made in the text, published in the fourteenth century, represented nothing new, but were cobbled together from the *Seventeen Tantras* by Rabjam. Hence, the Instruction Series, rather than representing an evolutionary advancement in Dzogchen beyond the Mind Series and the Space Series, was, and is, about promoting recycled, remedial, tantric twaddle as the pinnacle of Dzogchen.

The *togal* practices, as described by the *Tantras* and Rabjam, include self-massage, self-application of pressure points, postures, visualizations, and gazing exercises. Rabjam writes:

> The *key point* for practice as stated in the *Reverberation of Sound*: "It is a key point to press upon the luminosity of the bindu. Not moving the thumbs and index fingers from the channels, wisdom will increase."
>
> Thus as the quote continues [from the *Blazing Luminosity*]: "By pressing the index fingers and thumbs at the sockets of the eyes and next to them, have confidence that the [luminosity] will be rendered directly evident."

Bindu is a synonym for *thigle* in Dzogchen and means a small point or a sphere (sometimes described as the size of a thumbnail) that is luminous and without discernible edges. First off, how can someone press upon the luminosity of a *bindu*? It makes no sense. Moreover, it is unmitigated hooey to assume that such pressing will increase one's wisdom. Pressing one's eyes sockets and next to them, especially in a dark room, might cause one to see lights, or "luminosity," but such seeing has nothing whatsoever to do with true en-Light-enment.

I'll now quote Rabjam from the text:

> Here the key point, is, when pressing the light channels, appearances of light will dawn. It [the tantra *Vajrasattva's Mirror of the Heart*] states: "With the ways of gazing, the postures, the pressing the light channels at the side of the head, visions will fill the entire sky. This is the genuine seal for the quintessential, profound instructions."

Seeing visions that fill the entire sky (which one couldn't see with closed eyes) has nothing to do with "quintessential, profound instructions." Moreover, it's pure hyperbole to describe these visions as "filling the entire sky."

Three postures—the posture of the *Dharmakaya*, the posture of the *Sambhogakaya*, and the posture of the *Nirmanakaya*—are taught in the text, but to anyone with discernment, it is clear that these postures have nothing to do with the *Kayas*, nor do they yield the realizations claimed for them. Here's Rabjam's description of the posture of the *Dharmakaya*:

> The way of implementing the posture is like the pose of a lion. Placing the soles of the feet upon the ground is a key point for balancing the heat aspect of the elements. Posing by stretching the chest upward in the demeanor of a lion is the key point for increasing the wisdom wind and suppressing the karmic winds. Drawing the fingers and placing the fists upon the ground is the key point for reversing the movement of the karmic winds. Extending the upper torso and pulling the shoulders back is a key point for the

experience of the visions to swiftly arise. Inducing the strength of the neck is a key point for resting in inseparable space-wisdom... The qualities derived from striking these key points are mentioned in the *Golden Garuda*: "Whoever rests in the posture of the dharmakaya and applies the key point of the body correctly will experience the exaltation of dharmakaya."

No physical posture produces the experience of the *Dharmakaya*. But the *Golden Garuda* makes an even more outrageous claim for the posture of the *Nirmanakaya*, which is simply a squatting posture:

> To purify the collections of the body, whoever relies upon the key point for knowing and implementing the posture of the nirmanakaya will fully awaken and be liberated in that life.

In addition to *Dharmakaya*, *Sambhogakaya*, and *Nirmanakaya* postures, the *Tantras* also teach *Dharmakaya*, *Sambhogakaya*, and *Nirmanakaya* gazes. Rabjam writes:

> The three eyes correspond to the three ways of gazing. According to their order: since the dharmakaya has the eyes of the dharmata, the gaze is upward; the sambhogakaya has wisdom eyes, so the gaze is directly out; the nirmanakaya has the prajna eyes, so the gaze is downward. By directly seeing through the eyes of the dharmata, the nature will be determined right then and there.

These gazes, along with others prescribed in *togal*, such as flame-gazing and sun-gazing, have no correlation whatsoever with the *Kayas*. Moreover, it is laughable to associate the *Dharmakaya* gaze with the eyes of the *Dharmata*. One can only experience the *Dharmata* by being consciously present and at-one with the *Sambhogakaya*, the Clear-Light continuum. Then *Dharmata*, Being-Consciousness-Radiance, stands out as the Real, the unmanifest Condition underlying and transcending all manifest conditions.

Per Rabjam and the *Tantras*, experiencing and increasing wisdom and *Dharmata* can be accomplished merely through touch. Rabjam writes, "Those who accomplish wisdom should revitalize and apply pressure to the key points of the body." He then quotes *The Reverberation of Sound*, which states:

> To increase the dharmata, apply massage substances; and for the bindus, rely upon the body and wisdom.

It's hard to believe that anyone who endorses the Great Perfection would buy practices of gazes, postures, self-pressure, and self-massage to induce visions as the pinnacle of Dzogchen.

It just proves that real intelligence, discrimination, and honesty don't necessarily correlate with high-end Dharma. Why don't we see any lamas making the arguments that I do? Because Dzogchen is an insular tradition, and anyone who did would be, or would have been, excommunicated from the cult, and not only lose the benefits of membership, but face censure from the sect.

Why wouldn't students denounce these practices?

First, few were, or are, sharp enough to see through and deconstruct the teachings; second, the tradition threatens those who expose and criticize these so-called "secret" teachings or their teachers with a hell that rivals Christianity's. Rabjam, in *Precious Treasury of the Genuine Meaning*, elaborates the (putative) pitfalls of breaking *samaya* (meaning the vows or precepts that create a bond between the guru and disciple):

> The specific distinctions are threefold: disrespecting the guru, disrespecting the vajra family and exposing the secret [meaning the togal teachings]. First there is no limit to the faults derived through breaking samaya with the guru. In *Dynamic Strength*, it states: "The initial signs of losing samaya will be various degrees of unhappiness. Contagious and death-threatening diseases, as well as incurable diseases, will befall the person. Demonic forces and perverted spirits will take away life and the perpetrator will fall to the hells. Eyesight and hearing will be lost and nothing meaningful accomplished. Diseases such as leprosy and pox will be contracted. Thieves will bring harm, rulers will impose punishment, and other unknown illnesses will occur.
>
> To disrespect the guru is like, for example, extinguishing every light within a room so that nothing at all can be seen thereafter. One will remain in the lowest, most unbearable hell indefinitely to endure great suffering for many kalpas.

Unsurprisingly, however, other teachings in the text contradict the aforesaid dire warnings. For example, the *Sixfold Expanse* states, "There is no environment, so no teacher; and with no dharma, there is no retinue to receive teachings." And the *Dynamic Strength of the Lion* enjoins us to "Let go of the rigid mental idea of right or wrong."

If there is no teacher, no dharma, and no right or wrong, that renders the idea of losing *samaya* moot.

Are there other such contradictions in the text?

Plenty. For example, Rabjam argues that the *Alaya* and the *Dharmakaya* are not the same Ocean of Conscious. He writes: "Concerning this, in some sutras and tantras, the basic ground is labeled 'alaya.' Interpreting this, some scholars fail to capture the wisdom intent and instead assert that the alaya and dharmakaya are one and the same." But elsewhere in *Precious Treasury of the Genuine Meaning*, to emphasize that all phenomena have the same root, he quotes the *Reverberation of Sound*, which states: "The intrinsic nature of these confused appearances is wisdom previously unseen. Given that confusion and conceptualization are baseless, the alaya is realized to be the great dharmakaya."

But the most grievous contradiction is the one between the *Precious Treasury of the Genuine Meaning* and Rabjam's two most revered texts, *The Precious Treasury of the Way of Abiding* and *A Treasure Trove of Scriptural Transmission: A Commentary on The Precious Treasury of the Basic Space of Phenomena*. If you read these two texts (which extol the virtues of *trekcho*) and compare them to *Precious Treasury of the Genuine Meaning* (which denigrates *trekcho*), you might, like me, wonder how the same person could write such incongruent texts.

Let's first consider *A Treasure Trove of Scriptural Transmission: A Commentary on The Precious Treasury of the Basic Space of Phenomena*. In the text, translator Richard Barron (a.k.a. Lama Chokyi Nyima) writes:

> The *Choying Dzod [The Precious Treasury of the Basic Space of Phenomena]* focuses on the great perfection approach of trekcho, or "cutting through solidity," within the framework of view, meditation, conduct, and fruition. In the present volume, Longchen Rabjam writes that trekcho is the "ultimate meaning of the ground of being, which brings the most excellent individuals, those of the very highest acumen, to freedom effortlessly."

As Barron states, the text focuses on the effortless path of *trekcho*. And throughout the text, Rabjam continually quotes tantras that apotheosize *trekcho* as the pinnacle of Dzogchen. The tantra he most quotes is the *All-Creating Monarch* (*Kunjed Gyalpo*), the "fundamental tantra of Dzogchen," per Namkhai Norbu. Here's a typical *All-Creating Monarch* quote from Rabjam's text:

> Enlightenment, which is like space, will not come about for those who indulge in effort and achievement. Engaging in effort and achievement constitutes error and obscuration.

But in *Precious Treasury of the Genuine Meaning*, Rabjam reverses course, disparaging (effortless) *trekcho* while exalting (effortful) *togal*. In a subchapter of the book, titled "The Way Togal Surpasses Trekcho," he provides misrepresentations and faulty arguments to support his claim for the superiority of *togal*. For example, he writes: "With trekcho, wisdom is pursued through the projection of the conceptual mind; whereas here [through togal], it is recognized that the radiance of the nonconceptual awareness of clear light arises through the eyes. Hence this is surpassing."

First, it is, by Rabjam, a gross and blatant misrepresentation of *trekcho* to describe it as the pursuit of wisdom "through the projection of the conceptual mind." Anyone familiar with *trekcho* will patently reject his description. Second, it is wrong to assert that "clear light arises through the eyes." Clear Light, the radiant effulgence of the *Dharmakaya*, exists independently of one's eyes. Moreover, since it is clear, or transparent, it can't be seen with one's eyes, but can only be felt-perceived through the medium of consciousness itself. Hence, a yogi can experience it with his eyes closed.

A clear-headed mystic will reject the *Reverberation of Sound*'s statement "The key point of wisdom will originate through the eyes." But not the foggy Rabjam, who argues that eye-based wisdom makes *togal* superior to *trekcho*. He writes, "The difference based on the direct realization of the key points [of togal] is that, in trekcho, wisdom is not directly witnessed." Unbeknownst to Rabjam, wisdom is not an object; hence it can't be witnessed.

Rabjam writes that "Togal appearances are pure wisdom phenomena; and just by seeing them, the door to taking birth in the six realms will be closed." Because he holds these appearances, or visions, in high esteem, he promotes their proliferation. He writes:

> The difference based on the experience increasing is that, with trekcho, the way of cutting through the continuity of ordinary cognition is stabilized. Aside from that, the inner experience of the many aspects of samadhi—including clairvoyance, omniscience, and outer experience of visions such as lights and kayas—are not found. Here [with togal], the exceptional visionary experiences are ever-increasing.

First, the idea that *togal*-based *samadhis* produce clairvoyance and omniscience is just more Instruction Series hooey. Second, the experience of *Kayas* is inner and intradivine, not outer and visionary. One might see lights, among other objects, while meditating, but none of these objects are spiritual. Rather, when given any import, they represent spiritual materialism.

Beyond the fact that the togal *visions have no spiritual import, what can you say about them?*

First, they contradict the meditation experiences described in every other mystical tradition, which alone makes them suspect; second, they can, and have been, explained as physiological, rather than spiritual, phenomena; third, they reflect cultural conditioning; fourth, the claims of powers they grant are laughable; and fifth, the whole point of them is contradicted by statements in the text describing all appearances as "without substance."

The essence of the visions sought by *togal* practitioners revolves around *bindus*, which, as I earlier stated, are small, luminous points or spheres without discernible edges. These *bindus*, or *thigle*, as they are often referred to in Dzogchen, combine to form what are called *vajra* chains. And per *togal* teachings, the connected *thigle* make up the various forms of all "external" objects of reality. But, as I will argue, the *thigle* are simply visionary phenomena and not, as *togal* teachings claim, the indestructible building blocks of reality.

Bindus are poorly, superficially, and contradictorily explained in *Precious Treasury of the Genuine Meaning*. It is beyond the scope of our discussion to consider all the varying, unclear, and untenable statements made about them by Rabjam and the tantras he quotes. So, our consideration of them will be limited.

Rabjam identifies three types of *bindus*—relative, genuine, and natural—and correlates them with the three channels: *rasana* (right), *lalana* (left), and *avadhuti* (central). He writes:

> Specifically, within the rasana [channel], there is the nature of upaya as the causal relative bindu, characteristic of contaminated bliss. Within the lalana is the genuine wisdom bindu, characteristic of the bliss of immaculate prajna. Within the avadhuti is the natural dharmata bindu as spontaneously present clear light, the nature of indivisible space and wisdom.

The *rasana* channel is associated with sex and sexual fluid; so, per Rabjam, it is characteristic of "contaminated" bliss. Therefore, he emphasizes that genuine *bindus* are the path. He writes, "The relative are not the main path of practice here… Genuine bindus are the actual path." And genuine *bindus*, as he makes clear, produce the desired *togal* visions. He explains:

> In reliance upon genuine bindus, the empty nature of the dharmakaya will be realized. Train in the dynamic strength of awareness by stimulating the luminosity of the empty bindus. When familiarity occurs throughout the day and night, visions will effortlessly appear as the extent of accomplishment."

I have a question: If the central channel, the avadhuti, *is the* Dharmata bindu, *why isn't that the path rather than the genuine* bindus, *because the whole point of* togal *is to realize* Dharmata?

Good question, and the fact that it isn't directly the focus of practice shows that *togal* is not a direct path, but an indirect, visionary one. The central channel is the pathway of Clear Light, which cannot be seen; so no direct path could be a visionary one.

Rabjam talks of "stimulating the luminosity of the empty bindus." *How is this accomplished?*

Primarily through applied pressure. Here again is the quote he cites on this from the *Blazing Luminosity*:

It is a key point to press upon the luminosity of the bindu. Not moving the thumbs and index fingers from the channels, wisdom will increase.

By pressing the index fingers and thumbs at the sockets of the eyes and next to them, have confidence that the [luminosity] will be rendered directly evident.

How can pressing on the luminosity of a bindu *increase wisdom? That's like saying if you press on the light from a light bulb, that will affect the bulb. And how would pressing on the sockets of the eyes make the luminosity evident?*

Indeed, pressing on the luminosity of a *bindu* makes no sense, and thinking it will increase wisdom makes even less. I could cite and deconstruct hundreds of similarly absurd statements from the book, but then our *togal* consideration would go on for days. Pressing on the sockets of the eyes and next to them, and also on the neck (as described elsewhere in the text), no doubt precipitates and intensifies the visions; but, as I will argue, these visions are simply induced photic phenomena, not spiritual visions.

In our discussion of the visions and the esoteric anatomy that underpins them, meaning the lamps, light channels, and *chakras*, I will also cite Jigme Lingpa's *Yeshe Lama* and Christopher Hatchell's *Naked Seeing*. If you read Rabjam's *Precious Treasury of the Genuine Meaning*, which is a veritable tome, and then Lingpa's *Yeshe Lama,* which is about one-tenth its length, you will recognize the latter as essentially a condensation of the practices in the former. Here's how noted Dzogchen author Keith Dowman, who has translated the text into English, describes it:

> Here is the great Yeshe Lama, the most renowned, comprehensive, and efficacious of the Dzogchen manuals. It is a sourcebook for Dzogchen Breakthrough/Leapover precepts. Certainly, the Yeshe Lama lives up to its reputation. It is still the crown jewel of the latter-day Dzogchen lineages. It is at the apex of the Longchen Nyingtik corpus of literature, presenting the essential Dzogchen yogas in pith instruction. The Longchen Nyingtik is based firmly in Longchen Rabjampa's vision, a massive, vast and profound Dzogchen vision written down as the Seven Treasuries, which in turn were based intimately upon the tantras of the Nyingma Gyubum, the treasure house of Dzogchen.

My suggestion to those interested in *togal* is to first read *Yeshe Lama*. If it floats your boat, then dish out (at this time $45) for *Precious Treasury of the Genuine Meaning*. If you Google Yeshe Lama, you will find the Lama Chonam and Sangye Khandro translation available for free online. This is the version I will quote in my consideration.

For those who want to deeply consider the nature of *togal* visions, I highly recommend Professor Richard Hatchell's *Naked Seeing*, an outstanding academic text on visionary Buddhism that focuses primarily on *togal*.

Now to the visions. Because this isn't a course or a book, and because the visions are ultimately insignificant (as Rabjam himself points out), I'll cite just a few descriptions of them. Here are some from *Precious Treasury of the Genuine Meaning*, with my comments following:

> The practice of the ocean [i.e. eyes] involves the three key points concerning the way of gazing, as well as the postures and winds. Rather than pressing on the eyeballs with three fingers, only use two. In doing so, initially reddish [appearances] will seem to occur, followed by greenish-yellow, then blue, ablaze with their light. When the luminosity of the actual empty bindu arises as clear reddish-orange, apply pressure with the fingers for a while; and then gaze without wandering from that appearance. Then, letting go with the fingers, gaze while holding the ocean still. Again, when those appearances vanish, press down on the eyes and allow phenomena to become calm.

When your spiritual practice depends on pressing on your eyeballs with two fingers rather than three in order to induce certain visions—and the practice is claimed by its masters (such as Rabjam) to be the pinnacle of Dzogchen rather than the low-level tantra that it is—then you know that the tradition is corrupt.

Rabjam continues:

> The *actual practice* is that—at the point above the eyebrows—from the all-pervasive great blue light within the self-radiant light of five colors, bindus with lotus petals and so forth appear encircled by rainbow-light aura enclosure. This is called the "space enclosure" or the "appearance of the space of rainbow light." The blueness is called the self-nature of space.

The rainbow, or five-colored, light visions involving *bindus* (or *thigle*) are exalted in *togal*, and when, later in our discussion, we consider their nature, I will argue that they, like all other visions, are photic rather than spiritual in nature.

Rabjam writes:

> The indeterminate empty forms [of togal] will have no limit and appear as various kayas of the deities, the six classes of beings, faraway lands, islands on the ocean, realms of gods and others, patterns, stupas, lotuses, demons, corpses, multidimensional mountains, and so forth. Ineffable phenomena will emerge in this way due to the inner winds having gathered within the impure channels. This can be reversed by adjusting the way of gazing.
>
> Furthermore, when the light channels are pure, then unimpeded, faraway locations will be seen, as well as attaining the capacity to directly pass through the walls of the meditation hut to arrive outside.

The fact that merely altering one's way of gazing changes the visions one sees is evidence that the phenomena are optical illusions rather than real objects. So, one is not seeing "faraway lands" and "islands on the ocean," but just imagining that he is. If you believe that *togal* practitioners can pass through the walls of their meditation huts, then you're on blue spiritual pills, not red ones.

Rabjam quotes the *Reverberation of Sound*:

> Rather than pressing with the three [fingers], using the index finger and thumb, press upon the luminosity of the empty bindu. Due to the pressure, whatever emerges will be the vision of the direct realization of the dharmata.

It is farcical to claim that the pressure of one's finger and thumb on the luminosity of a *bindu* will induce a vision of the direct realization of the *Dharmata*, which is Being-Consciousness. One can only have a "vision," or experience, of Being-Consciousness by be-ing it, which has nothing to do with any visual experience.

Rabjam then cites *Blazing Luminosity*:

> With the index finger and thumb in the sockets of the eyes and next to them, the actual visions will be induced. Trusting this [method] means self-liberation will be effortless.

Anyone who thinks that sticking their index finger and thumb in their eye sockets to induce visions will make self-liberation effortless is either spiritually clueless or brainwashed.

Here's a sample from *Yeshe Lama* describing some of the more exotic visions a *togal* practitioner might experience:

> Once the wisdom of the sambhogakaya reaches its full extent, all five buddha families—such as the conqueror Akshobhya—appear as solitary figures, then with complete ornamentation, and then with consorts in their fully perfected aspect. The principal ones and their retinues arise distinctly in group formations and are surrounded by the mandala's

vajra fence and so forth, originating from the immaculate purification of the dharmakaya. The vision is so perfectly clear that ordinary phenomena are naturally arrested. Wherever cognition is directed, it is able to penetrate so inanimate forms are set into motion and even the body can be seen as partless particles. Mountains, crags, and other solid formations [can be penetrated] free from obstruction.

Visions of Buddha families and their retinues and consorts are culturally conditioned. *Togal* practitioners not inculcated with Buddhist dogma would not experience such visions; hence they have nothing to do with the "immaculate purification of the dharmakaya." Just as Christians have visions of Jesus and angels, *togal* practitioners experience appearances of Buddhist-related phenomena.

The claim that directed cognition can penetrate and set into motion inanimate forms, such as mountains and crags, is utter hooey. Moreover, *togal* practitioners do not see objects and bodies as "partless particles," because such particles do not exist. The idea of the "atom" (or partless particle) as the irreducible "building block" of material entities has long been debunked by modern physics. Though partless particles were postulated by the ancients, no one has seen them. The Dzogchen idea that *thigle*, which are mere visionary phenomena, are this partless particle, is pure poppycock. And the fact that *thigle* are sometimes described as the size of a thumbnail makes this idea even more preposterous.

What is the point of these togal *visions? How can Dzogchen justify them as the pinnacle of their path?*

Their point is to lead the yogi beyond them. This is called "the vision of the exhaustion of the dharmata," which means "the clearing of visionary experiences." Therefore, as Rabjam himself says, "These visions have no innate, true existence"; hence, the "exhaustion of the dharmata," is, in his words, "simply the ultimate fruition."

The fact that these visions have no true existence, and nothing to do with *Dharmata*, begs the question as to why they are exalted by the *Seventeen Tantras*, the Instruction Series, and Rabjam. As I've previously stated, because few Dzogchen practitioners can properly practice *rigpa*, Dzogchen was impelled to provide an alternative path, and a visionary tantric one was chosen because it is alluring and mystical, which it had to be for Dzogchen to compete with other Tibetan traditions. Then, to promote it, they had to exaggerate its spiritual status by making outlandish claims for the powers it grants, because that's what competing traditions did.

Although I can understand why Dzogchen apotheosized its *togal* teachings, I can only identify them as the perversion of true *togal*, or leap-over. And I contend that if true *togal* (meaning Spirit contemplation and conductivity) were properly taught, then the bastardized orthodox version would not have to be.

What can you say about the cause or basis for the visions?

I know little about entoptic (or eye-sourced) phenomena, but if you Google the subject, you will find that it's not uncommon for ordinary people to see visions akin to those described in *togal*. You will find web pages by eye doctors that describe all kinds of visual phenomena that people experience under different conditions (such as in the dark) or when their eyes, for various reasons, are not functioning normally (which is the case when one presses on one's eye sockets). There is even a condition called "rainbow vision" wherein people see rainbow circles around light, which matches descriptions of *thigle*.

Naked Seeing by Christopher Hatchell, which I mentioned earlier, is the book to get if you want to deeply consider the nature of *togal* visions. Here's a sample excerpt wherein Hatchell cites a Harvard blindfolding experiment:

> Some studies have focused on inducing similar imagery in subjects with intact visual systems by placing them in total visual deprivation, a context that would mimic that of dark-retreat. A blindfolding experiment conducted at Harvard Medical School, for instance, placed thirteen subjects in specially constructed blindfolds that allowed the eyes to move freely but blocked out all light. The subjects remained blindfolded for five days and were given tape recorders to allow them to document their experiences. Unsurprisingly, the reports by the blindfolded subjects correlate closely with literary accounts of visionary experiences in dark-retreat: the onset of visual experiences as unstructured spots

and patches of light (called "phosphenes"), which for many subjects eventually turned into complex, realistic experiences like peacock feathers, faces, architecture, and landscapes.

Now, let's turn our attention to the "esoteric anatomy" described by the *Seventeen Tantras* and Longchen Rabjam. This means the channels, *chakras*, luminosities, and elements. Because the descriptions of this "anatomy" by the *Tantras* and Rabjam are not always clear or in agreement, I welcome corrections to my commentary.

Let's start with the channels. The *Tantras* and Rabjam recognize the same three main channels as Hindu yoga: *sushumna* (central), *ida* (left), and *pingala* (right). The Tibetan terms for these channels are *avadhuti*, *lalana*, and *rasana*. In addition to these "basic" channels, the *Tantras* posit four, and sometimes five, "wisdom light" (or luminous) channels that originate in the heart and join in or are contained in the central channel. But as Christopher Hatchell states in *Naked Seeing*, "The canonical texts do not all agree on the names and functions of the luminous channels."

The commonly described four "wisdom light" channels are the Great Golden Kati, the Crystal Pipe, the White Silken Thread, and the Slender Coil. And in some *Tantras*, a fifth channel, the Empty Self-Liberated (which we will not consider), is also recognized. Even though these channels are clearly differentiated from the three main channels, the *Tantras* sometimes refer to "the four channels"—the three main channels plus the Crystal Pipe. Clearly, the Crystal Pipe, sometimes referred to as the Crystal Kati, has a special status among the luminous channels, and we'll consider it after I briefly describe the other channels.

The White Silken Thread and the Slender Coil are two branches of a single channel that originates in the heart and terminates in the eyes. The branch that connects the heart to the right eye is the Silken Thread, while the other branch, the Slender Coil, leads to the left eye. This two-pronged channel putatively functions "to produce outer appearances."

Only a couple of sentences in *Precious Treasury of the Genuine Meaning* describe the Great Golden Kati channel, and these descriptions are vague. From what I can gather from the book and a web search, this channel functions as a matrix, or "container," for the Clear Light itself, the Crystal Pipe. In other words, the "pipe," or "plumbing," is the Great Golden Kati channel, while the Clear-Light energy that courses through it is the Crystal Pipe, or Crystal Kati.

Regarding the relation of the four "wisdom light" channels to the central channel (*avadhuti*), Rabjam writes:

> Concerning this, the names [of the channels] are: the great golden kati channel; crystal pipe with hollow interior; the white silken thread, or the slender coil; and the great empty self-liberated channel. These four gateways are self-appearing channels. Becoming the path, they join the central channel.

But not all Dzogchen masters associate the Crystal Kati with the central channel. Consider this excerpt from the book *Natural Liberation: Padmasambhava's Teachings on the Six Bardos*:

> In all treatises other than the *Tantra of the Sun of the Clear Expanse of the Great Perfection* and the *Profound Dharma of the Natural Emergence of the Peaceful and Wrathful from Enlightened Awareness*, the hollow crystal kati channel is kept secret, and there are no discussions of this special channel of primordial wisdom. This channel is unlike the central channel, the right channel, the left channel, or any of the channels of the five chakras; it is absolutely not the same as any of them. Its shape is like that of a peppercorn that is just about open, there is no blood or lymph inside it, and it is limpid and clear. A special technique for opening this is hidden in the instructions on the natural liberation pertaining to the lower orifice, great bliss, and desire. The lower yanas do not have even the name of this channel.

So, do you consider the Crystal Kati Tube to be in or part of the central channel?

I consider it to be an extension of the basic central channel, the *sushumna* in Hindu yoga. I envision it as extending from the crown to the spiritual Heart-center, located and felt-experienced two digits to the right of center of one's chest. From my perspective, it is the same Light-Energy current as *Atma Nadi*, a.k.a. *Amrita Nadi*, which some yogis consider to be the true *sushumna*, or central channel.

I don't think Dzogchen acknowledges the right side of the heart as the locus for the Crystal Kati.

Dzogchen's "esoteric anatomy" doesn't acknowledge many things that are esoterically important. If it did, Dzogchen texts would identify the Kati Tube not as a tube or pipe, but as a force-current with a concomitant field of light surrounding it. It would identify it as the "pathway" of the immanent *Sambhogakaya*.

If you want to know how clueless Dzogchen masters can be regarding esoteric anatomy, consider this statement made by Jigme Lingpa: "Mind is located in a channel in the lungs. While wisdom is located in the physical heart."

My suggestion for students is to compare Dzogchen's "esoteric anatomy," which I have little affinity for, with Ramana Maharshi's and Adi Da's, which I resonate with. We could spend days comparing esoteric anatomies, including Hindu tantra's, but that would lead us outside the scope of our *togal* consideration.

Dzogchen only recognizes four chakras.

Correct. Its "esoteric anatomy" only accounts for the crown, throat, heart, and navel *chakras*, and it doesn't explain them clearly or deeply. I cannot respect an esoteric-anatomy system that doesn't account for the *Ajna* (or third-eye) *chakra*, because such a system cannot properly explain en-Light-enment. The *Ajna chakra* is a crucial "doorway" to Awakening, because it is the final and toughest *pranic* "knot" to pierce. This is so because four cardinal *pranic* channels intersect and intertwine at this locus. And until this *Ajna* "door" is opened to a threshold degree, Light-Energy from above cannot descend into the Heart-center (*Hridayam*), wherein a *bodhisattva* is "converted" into a Buddha. And until this "door" is fully opened, one cannot attain Buddhahood.

Most importantly, this *chakra* can only be opened through Grace, meaning *Shaktipat*, the descent of Divine Power. Divine Power, or *Shakti*, is the same Light-Energy Body as the *Sambhogakaya*. And only the descent, or "pouring down," of the *Sambhogakaya*, called *Dharmamegha*, can "produce," or unveil, *Dharmata*, the Suchness of Buddhahood. When the Heart-center knot is severed by this *Shakti*, then *Bodhicitta* ensues.

Why doesn't Dzogchen account for Dharmamegha?

It periodically, cryptically alludes to it, but fails to incorporate it into its core Dharma. Here's a quote of Longchen Rabjam, excerpted from Sam van Schaik's *Approaching the Great Perfection*: "The heart essence of the teaching is not [given out] at the door; it is necessary that the transmission of the truth descends into one's heart." I can't explain why Dzogchen fails to account for *Shaktipat*, culminating in *Dharmamegha*, as the focus of its *togal* teachings, but because it does, I was moved to present my own version of "spontaneous presence."

What about the luminosities and elements? Are you going to discuss them?

Yes, right now, in fact. We got off track when the subject of *Dharmamegha* came up, and now we're back on. I'll start with the Four Luminosities that Dzogchen identifies: the Far-reaching Water Luminosity, the Empty Bindu Luminosity, the Luminosity of Perfectly Pure Basic Space, and the Luminosity of Self-Emergent Prajna. I'm not going to spend much time discussing them, because they are just more of the same convoluted, contradiction-laden rubbish that infests canonical *togal* teachings.

In *Precious Treasury of the Genuine Meaning*, Longchen Rabjam provides what he calls a "detailed description of the location from which the four luminosities emerge [i.e., the eyes]." He writes:

> First, from the right eye, two of the luminosities—namely, the water luminosity of the far-reaching lasso and the luminosity of self-emergent prajna—arise as the upaya [means] of appearances, or the wisdom that knows the way things appear. From the left eye, two luminosities—namely the luminosity of the empty bindu and the luminosity of perfectly pure space—arise as the prajna of emptiness, or the wisdom that knows the nature of things just as they are.

The idea that self-emergent *prajna* (wisdom) emerges from the right eye is ludicrous. If this were the case, a yogi with no right eye could not experience self-emergent *prajna,* and a blind yogi could not experience any luminosities.

The Water Luminosity of the Far-reaching Lasso is simply the "eye that can catch distant objects." This "luminosity" has nothing to do with the right eye, and is dependent on external physical light, or "luminosity."

Nowhere in *Precious Treasury of the Genuine Meaning* does Rabjam satisfactorily clarify what the empty *bindu* is. The term *bindu* can have multiple meanings. It can refer to a tiny point or dot or sphere of light, or to an edgeless expanse. But if it's empty without edges, how can one see it? And what's confusing is that in some places in the text, rather than a single empty *bindu* being described (though unclearly), multiple empty *bindus* are referred to. For example, Rabjam cites the *Reverberation of Sound*, which says, "Train in the dynamic strength of awareness by stimulating the luminosity of the empty bindus." Elsewhere he cites the *Blazing Luminosity*, which claims that "the luminosity of the empty bindu represents the basis of all phenomena." Then he references the *Reverberation of Sound*, which states: "The characteristics of the empty bindu are that it is round and naturally all-illuminating. It arises, radiating with light the color of red." How can a mere vision that arises (which means that it also subsides) represent the basis of all phenomena, especially when elsewhere in *Precious Treasury of the Genuine Meaning* we are told that all "these astonishing appearances are without substance"? Only in "counterfeit" Dzogchen, meaning standard *togal* teachings.

The descriptions of the luminosity of perfectly pure basic space in *Precious Treasury of the Genuine Meaning* are, in a word, farcical. Here's one that Rabjam cites from *Blazing Luminosity*:

> The luminosity of perfectly pure space gathers the nature of awareness so that it appears in the enclosure of the vajra chain. Whoever becomes familiar with this will see it as the self-clarity of unchanging blue light abiding in the enclosure of an aura of light. Self-clarity then appears as the outer objective sphere.

The idea that the luminosity of space gathers the nature of awareness is absurd, as is the idea that self-clarity appears as the outer objective sphere.

Rabjam then cites the tantra the *Garden of Pearls*, which says, "Since the objective sphere of the dharmata is perfectly pure, it arises from the corners of both eyes." Then, he cites the *Reverberation of Sound* again, which states, "From the corners [of the eyes], the two kayas [the dharmakaya and rupakaya] are sustained; and the all-encompassing phenomena will then increase."

The objective sphere does not arise from the corners of one's eyes; it exists independently, or "objectively," apart from one's eyes. As I said earlier in our discussion, the idea that the two *Kayas* are sustained from the corners of the eyes is laughable. The *Kayas* have nothing whatsoever to do with one's eyes. Regarding the increase of "all-encompassing phenomena," why would a yogi seek this when the goal is the "exhaustion of Dharmata," the clearing of visionary experiences?

Now we'll consider the elements, yet another example of Dzogchen's muddled metaphysics. *Togal* teachings identify the same five elements as Hindu yoga—space, fire, earth, air, and water—but beyond this, they go off the rails. First, they are clueless regarding space. They not only fail to clearly differentiate between the space element and so-called "basic space," they also fail to identify the space element as the *Akasha*, or ether. And unbeknownst to them, the other four elements derive from the space element, the ether, and not from the five lights (blue, white, yellow, red, and green). Those with insight into the elements can only laugh at Rabjam's ignorance when he states, "Hence, due to the presence of these five lights, the five elements emerge at the present time." Those who understand Hindu yogic *tattvas* (the hierarchical constituent principles or evolutes of existence) know that colors are not *tattvas* whose presence begets the elements. Moreover, as science informs us, the color of an object only indicates the wavelength of light it reflects.

So, the five elements are not the five lights as claimed by Dzogchen?

Correct. And Dzogchen's association of the five elements with specific colors has no basis in reality, but is arbitrary. If you examine other wisdom traditions, such as Western alchemy and Chinese spirituality, you will find different correlations between the elements and colors.

Dzogchen also conflates the five elements with its five wisdoms (wisdom of the basic space of phenomena, mirrorlike wisdom, evenness wisdom, discerning wisdom, and all-accomplishing wisdom), and this too has no basis in reality. Furthermore, Dzogchen makes ridiculous statements pertaining to the element/wisdom relations. For example, in *Precious Treasury of the Genuine Meaning*, Rabjam cites the tantra *Self-Arising*, which states: "The five aspects of wind enhance wisdom's radiance; the five fire elements impel wisdom's strength; the five earth elements constitute wisdom's nature; the five water elements become the objects of wisdom; and the five space elements of space provide wisdom's dwelling place." And if you're wondering what the five-aspect divisions of the elements are like, here, as an example, is *Self-Arising*'s breakdown of earth: "The five divisions of earth are all-illuminating earth energy, unchanging vajra earth, precious source of all earth, appearances revealing completely limitless earth energy, and perfected earth energy."

I could continue to cite more Dzogchen poppycock pertaining to the elements, but because our discussion has already exceeded its scheduled time frame, we'll now move on to the claims of *siddhis* made for *togal* by Rabjam and some of the *Seventeen Tantras*. I'll list some of these claims, excerpted from *Precious Treasury of the Genuine Meaning*, and you can decide for yourself if they pass the smell test.

> Having reached this extent [of full enlightenment], there is the indication of perfection. All tangible appearances become complete, and the phenomenon of earth and matter dissolve. The mind is able to engage with anything, and the indication is that an inanimate object can be brought to life. [from the *Reverberation of Sound*]

At that time [of full enlightenment], the mind will be cognizant with six states of clairvoyance. All phenomena will be instantly known, whether far away or covertly hidden. [from the *Reverberation of Sound*]

Those who are familiar with the sounds of the elements and languages of the six classes will not be harmed by the elements. This includes not being burned by fire, not sinking or drowning in water, not touching the earth, and possessing the potential to pass through the sky. [from *Blazing Relics*]

This individual will be able to fly through the sky and, likewise, pass underground, as well as comprehend the meaning of that which is comprehensible or not… Having realized the mind to be empty, there will be potential to dissolve anything that is focused upon… Possessing deathless awareness the body will resemble a sixteen-year-old youth. [from *Blazing Relics*]

The practitioner will appear to be crazed, will be able to pass unimpeded through matter such as mountains and crags. Likewise, they would be capable of passing underground and through water, wander naked, and be unobstructed with whatever is encountered… Whoever becomes familiar with dharmakaya will, according to the field of others' perception, be physically invisible. Hence the practitioner will be free to do anything… The strength of the body will grant a previously unattained power of speed walking. Wrinkles will dissolve, and white hair will turn dark again. Becoming like a sixteen-year-old youth, the sheen of vitality will be possessed. [from *Blazing Relics*]

Through familiarity with emptiness, phenomena will be seen as particles; and it will then be possible to pass directly through fences, mountains, walls, and the like. Through magical powers, the body will elevate in space; and it is even said that the corpse will be cremated by its own wisdom fire. [by Longchen Rabjam]

Wow! What beyond-belief baloney. Do you consider Dzogchen's claims for the Rainbow Body to be just more of the same?

Yes. The hype for the Rainbow Body comes from the same *Tantras* that produced the above block of baloney. Since it's just another slice off the same block, why should anyone consider it different? Until I see it for myself or see documented scientific proof, I'm not buying the dissolution of the body into Light.

I'm confused. Namkhai Norbu writes that Dzogchen is all about attaining the Body of Light, meaning the Rainbow Body, which is only attainable through togal, *per Yeshe Lama. Yet, all his books are only about* trekcho. *And amazingly, he claims that Dzogchen is not tantra, when it clearly is.*

Although Norbu, who passed in 2018, was perhaps the most revered of the Tibetan masters who disseminated Dzogchen in the West, he was as Dharma-challenged and contradiction-riddled as Longchen Rabjam and Jigme Lingpa. Let's briefly consider his teachings on *togal* and the Body of Light. In his text *The Crystal and the Way of Light: Sutra, Tanta and Dzogchen*, he writes:

> But Dzogchen is neither sutra nor tantra. The basis for the communication of Dzogchen is introduction, not transformation into a manifestation as in tantra. And Dzogchen's principal practices work directly at the level of Mind in order to allow the individual to discover the primordial state to which he or she is introduced directly by the master, and to continue in it until the total realization of the Great Transfer or the Body of Light are achieved.

First, as you stated, it couldn't be clearer that Dzogchen is tantra. Not only is *togal* based on the *Seventeen Tantras*, but the foremost Mind-Series (*Semde*) text, *The Supreme Source* (or *All-Creating Monarch*), is, in Norbu's own words, "The Fundamental Tantra of the Dzogchen Semde." Secondly, Norbu asserts that working "directly at the level of Mind" will culminate in the "total realization of the Great Transfer or Body of Light." This contradicts standard Instruction Series (*Menngagde*) teachings, which state that, while *trekcho* enables a practitioner to attain the so-called "Rainbow Body," it is only *togal* that enables a practitioner's body to dissolve into Light, and thereby physically disappear.

Norbu, in the following passage from *The Crystal and the Way of Light*, describes *togal* (*thodgal*) as exceeding *trekcho* (*tregchod*):

> Continuing beyond Tregchod there is the practice of Thodgal, which means "surpassing the utmost", with the sense that "as soon as you're here, you're there". This practice is genuinely secret, and it is not appropriate to give more than the most basic description of it here. Thodgal is found only in the Dzogchen teachings. Through the practice of it

one is able to carry one's state of being rapidly to the ultimate goal. Through the development of the Four Lights, the Four Visions of Thodgal arise, and working with the inseparability of vision and emptiness one proceeds until the realization of the Body of Light is attained. This is the consummation of existence in which the physical body itself is dissolved into the essence of the elements, which is light.

Because Norbu, as made clear in this passage, identifies *togal* as superior to *trekcho*, the takeaway is that all of his books, none of which teach *togal,* are peddling an inferior practice in *trekcho*. Then, he contradicts himself when he says togal means "as soon as you're here, you're there," because later in the paragraph he describes the practice in terms of "development" (of the Four Lights). In other words, even though you are there, you are not really there, because you've yet to develop these lights. He concludes by describing the dissolution of the physical body into Light as the consummation of existence, but because he didn't publicly teach *togal*, every published text and talk of his was about less than this consummation.

Are the Four Visions experienced the same way in trekcho *as in* togal?

Before I answer your question, I'm going to quote Norbu on the Four Visions:

> The first of these Four Visions of Thodgal is called the 'Vision of Dharmata' (or 'nature of reality'), and the second vision is the further development of the first. The third is the maturation of it, and the fourth is the consummation of existence.

Per Norbu and other Dzogchen masters, the Four Visions of *Dharmata* are visions of Reality (*Dharmakaya*, or Mind)-as-Thusness, or Being-Consciousness. Those who practice *trekcho* must pass through these "visions," or stages, in order to attain consummate (meaning unbroken and unqualified) realization of *Dharmata* (and they do so by spontaneously transitioning to the practice of true *togal*, as I have described it). *Dharmata* has nothing whatsoever to do with appearances (of lights, *thigles*, rainbows, or anything else), and can only be realized through the (unborn, or non-phenomenal) *Trikaya*, which, as Norbu makes clear, is the base, path, and fruit of Dzogchen. Hence, these "visions" must be the same for all Dzogchen practitioners. Again, these "visions" are not visual, for it is only phenomenal appearances, which are not Reality, that can be seen.

Yogis in other traditions (including the other major gnostic Buddhist schools) practice the same direct, immediate presence as Dzogchen, and they experience the equivalent of the Four Visions; but they don't make the same claims for a Rainbow Body and the dissolution of one's body in Light. When one considers all the absurd and untenable claims made in the *Seventeen Tantras* and the *Precious Treasury of the Genuine Meaning*, it's logical to conclude that the Rainbow Body claims are just more of the same.

Where do you think Dzogchen got the idea of bodily dissolution in the Light?

Perhaps from the Catholic Church's teaching of transubstantiation, wherein bread and wine are vanished into the invisible Body of Christ. Dzogchen just carries the myth one step further by claiming the yogi himself dissolves in the Body of Light, which is the same hypostasis as the invisible Body of Christ. Given the numerous parallels between Dzogchen and Catholicism, this is a tenable assumption.

Summary

You've covered a lot of ground in your consideration of togal. *Can you summarize your view of standard* togal *teachings and compare these teachings to your own?*

Standard *togal* teachings employ special gazes, bodily postures, and techniques (such as squeezing the eyeballs and exerting pressure on the side of the neck) to induce/produce luminous visions. And these visions, which are mere appearances and not real (but just photic or entoptic phenomena), eventually exhaust themselves, ostensibly culminating in the realization of *Dharmata*.

My view is that these teachings are not (as claimed by the *Seventeen Tantras*, Longchen Rabjam, Jigme Lingpa, and other exponents of the Instruction Series) superior to *rigpa*, but inferior. In fact, they are not even true Dzogchen; rather, they are reductive yoga teachings not on the level of Ati (or Primordial) yoga. My view is that the exponents of standard *togal* teachings are shameless perverters of Great Perfection Teachings and outright liars who make outrageous and fallacious claims for their visionary yoga.

I'm not alone in my recognition of standard *togal* teachings as a reductive departure from the Great Perfection. In his *Approaching the Great Perfection*, author Sam van Schaik writes:

> The *Longchen Nyingtig* [the fundamental canonical *togal* teaching] represents both a graduated method and a gradual realization. It should be apparent that this wholly gradualist prescription stands in stark contrast to the discourse in the Great Perfection treasure texts, and that Jigme Lingpa employs the interpretive device of different levels of ability in practitioners in an attempt to reconcile this contradiction.

My view is that exponents of standard *togal* teachings lacked the insight and understanding to properly present and teach *rigpa*, the meditative enactment of the Great Perfection. Consequently, they resorted to remedial *togal* teachings and disingenuously promoted them as superior to *trekcho*, when, in fact, *trekcho* and (true) *togal* should be taught as the two complementary components of the single practice of *rigpa*.

My Electrical Spiritual Paradigm (ESP), which applies Ohm's Law to spirituality, properly identifies *trekcho* as the practice of maximal spiritual voltage (or force), and *togal* as the practice of spiritual amperage (or flow). As such, *trekcho* and *togal* are the two inseparable components of the En-Light-enment project. When *trekcho* is understood as the enactment, or the attempt at enactment, of Holy Communion, meaning attentional at-one-ment with the Holy Ghost (or Clear Light), and *togal* as the contemplation and conductivity (or reception) of the Holy

Ghost as Holy Spirit (or Clear-Light Energy), then the En-Light-enment project is understood. And when Clear-Light Energy (the Holy Spirit, or *Sambhogakaya*) permanently unites with one's *citta* (or soul, or consciousness) in the Heart-center, resulting in *Bodhicitta* (or Buddhahood), then the En-Light-enment project is consummated.

CHAPTER SEVEN

Electrical Dzogchen (Plugged-in Presence)

The Mechanics of Rigpa in Electrical Terms

In your book Electrical Christianity, *you elaborate your Plugged-in-Presence method. How does this method compare to Dzogchen?*

It could be described as Electrical Dzogchen because it explains the "mechanics" of *rigpa* (meaning *trekcho* and *togal*) in electrical terms, via my Ohm's Law paradigm. Because my text is Christian, I don't use Dzogchen terms in my description of Plugged-in Presence; but one can see the same terms expressed in other words. Also, my Plugged-in-Presence method does what Tibetan Dzogchen fails to do: it describes the practice of presence-oneness in detail, as a whole-bodily practice.

I'll now, via my Plugged-in Presence teaching (extracted from *Electrical Christianity*, but substituting in Dzogchen terms), describe Dzogchen in three related ways that make its electrical-like nature clear: first, via dialectic, then, via Ohm's Law, and last, via detailed practice instructions.

Dzogchen as a Dialectic

The practices of presence and absence constitute a dialectic, with presence (or relationship) as the *thesis*, absence (or inner emptiness) as the *antithesis*, and the descent of the *Sambhogakaya* (or Clear-Light Energy) as the *synthesis*. In other words, the pressure of the yogi's conscious presence (or relational force) instigates his self-emptying (or surrendering), which "produces," or pulls down, the *Sambhogakaya*, which deifies him, eventually transforming him into a Self (or Buddha)-realized being.

In engendering the descent of the *Sambhogakaya*, the two dialectical practices of presence (or relationship) and absence (or emptiness) give birth to a third, synthesizing practice: the practice of *power*. The practice of presence is about *connecting*; the practice of absence is about *surrendering*; and the practice of power, which integrates the practices of presence and absence, is about *receiving*.

The practice of receiving the *Sambhogakaya synthesizes* the practices of presence and absence by, in effect, *mediating* them. Thus, instead of full attention being focused on either the act of being present or the act of being self-empty, the act of receiving, or *conducting*, the *Sambhogakaya*, or Spirit-current, involves the artful integration of both these gestures. It involves the *letting go* of psychical content while simultaneously *holding on* to the context of connectedness. In order to instigate the drawing down of Divine Power, the *Sambhogakaya*, the yogi must sometimes emphasize the "pole of presence" (or relationship), and at other times the "pole of absence" (or self-emptying). But when the descent of Light-Energy is intense, the yogi can dispense with the dialectical spiritual practices (of presence and absence) and effortlessly rest in the Blessing/Blissing-current from above.

Ohm's Law and Dzogchen

The dialectical spiritual practice you've described does seem to mirror an electrical circuit, with the Sambhogakaya, *or Spirit-current, representing the amperage-like resolution of voltage-like conscious force and ohms-like reduced resistance. But how can you be sure that Ohm's Law applies to spirituality?*

No one can prove (or disprove) that Ohm's Law applies to Spirit-conductivity. But based on my own spiritual experiences, it is obvious to me that Ohm's Law, or some approximate variation of it, applies to the practice of *rigpa* (which breaks down to the practices of *trekcho* and *togal*, its constituent components). Consequently, even if Ohm's Law does not exactly hold true for the practices of *trekcho* (consciousness-force) and *togal* (Spirit-conductivity), it still provides a nonpareil metaphor for understanding the mechanics of *rigpa*.

For those of you unfamiliar with Ohm's Law, it states that "the strength or intensity of an unvarying electric current is directly proportional to the electromotive force and inversely proportional to the resistance in a circuit." Ohm's Law—where V = voltage (electromotive force), I = amperage (intensity of current), and R = ohms (units of resistance)—can be summarized in three formulas:

$$V = IR \; ; \; I = \frac{V}{R} \; ; \; R = \frac{V}{I}$$

(Note: Any form of the Ohm's Law equation can be derived from the other two via simple algebra.)

Translating Ohm's Law into a Dzogchen formula is simple. All we need to do is to substitute connected consciousness (or consciousness-force) for voltage, spiritual energy (or intensity of the Spirit-current) for amperage, and ego-resistance (or degree of resistance to the Spirit-current) for ohms. Therefore, the Electrical Dzogchen formula—where C = connected consciousness (or consciousness-force), I = spiritual energy (or intensity of the Spirit-current), and R = ego-resistance (or degree of resistance to the Spirit-current)—can, like Ohm's Law, be summarized in three formulas:

$$C = IR \; ; \; I = \frac{C}{R} \; ; \; R = \frac{C}{I}$$

(Note: As with Ohm's Law, any of these equations can be derived from the other two via simple algebra.)

Can you simplify and summarize the Ohm's Law/Dzogchen analogy?

Yes. *Trekcho* (Plugged-in Presence, or "Holy Communion") is the electromotive force (voltage), *togal* is conductivity (amperage) of the flow of the force as the Spirit-current (or *Sambhogakaya*), and ego-resistance is the resistance to the flow of the current (ohms). Ohm's Law applied to Dzogchen tells us that the intensity of the *Sambhogakaya's* flow is directly proportional to one's presence (or relational/communal) force and inversely proportional to the degree of one's ego-resistance (or self-grasping). Once you've been "initiated" by the Spirit (or *Sambhogakaya*), you'll be able to palpably and viscerally experience the seeming reality of Ohm's Law in Dzogchen spirituality.

The Sambhogakaya *is typically described as the Light, or Bliss, Body in Dzogchen. How is it that you correlate it with a Spirit-current?*

As I've stated in our previous talks, in some Buddhist literature the *Sambhogakaya* is described as the "Vehicle of Divine Power" and as "unceasing in nature." This identifies it as the dynamic Energy of the *Dharmakaya*. And when the yogi intensely receives this Energy, it is felt as a force-current being pulled down into the Heart-center (two-digits to the right of center of one's chest). This force-current, like an electric current, generates a concomitant force-field; and in the case of the *Sambhogakaya*, this field is experienced as radiant Light. Hence, the *Sambhogakaya* is best described as a Light-Energy Body rather than as just a Light Body. When the yogi rests in Heart-felt communion with this "Body," he spontaneously experiences bliss, which explains why it is also referred to as the "Bliss Body."

Practice Instructions

The following contemplation instructions are excerpted from my book *Electrical Christianity*. I've inserted some Buddhist terms (such as *Sambhogakaya*, Samantabhadra, and Adi Buddha) to make the instructions more "Dzogchen-friendly."

PLUGGED-IN PRESENCE INSTRUCTIONS

1) Sit upright, but relaxed, on a chair, bench, or meditation cushion.

2) Establish what the Buddha called "self-possession." In other words, feel yourself as the whole body, and then be consciously present as the whole body, the whole psycho-physical being. Randomly focusing your attention on your third-eye area and hands will enable you to coincide with your body, and thereby heal the body-mind split. When you consciously inhabit your whole body—and are wholly, or integrally, present to the whole (the totality of existence)—you are in proper position to receive and conduct the *Sambhogakaya* (or Holy Spirit), the Force-flow from above.

3) "Gaze" into empty space. If you are "self-possessed," this "gaze" will amount to being whole-bodily present to (or in direct relationship to) the void. As soon as you become aware that you have retracted from your "position" of conscious connectedness to (or single-pointed focus on) the void, simply reassume, or attempt to reassume, your "stance" of holistic at-one-ment. To this end, you can randomly use an enquiry (such

as "Avoiding relationship?") to instigate your resumption of communion with the void. When the void begins to "shine," it is experienced as Divine Presence. When the Power of the Presence pours down upon you, then "emptiness" has morphed into Spirit, and your "gaze into space" has transmuted into empowered Divine Communion.

4) Randomly focus your attention on your breath by being in direct relationship to your breathing cycle. When the breath "comes alive" as *prana-shakti*, or palpable intensified life-energy, simply remain present to it. Your communion with the breath cycle will transmute into true, or infused, Divine Communion when the *prana-shakti* morphs into the *Sambhogakaya—Anugraha-Shakti* poured down from above.

5) Totally relax your body (including your head) and utterly let go of your mind. Once you are able to connect to the *Shakti*, you will directly experience that letting go intensifies the force-flow (or pressure) of the Spirit-current. Be an empty cup, ready to be filled with Holy Water from above. When you experience the Benediction, the Divine downpour, remain motivelessly present to it. Your searchless beholding of the *Shakti* will enable you to spontaneously merge with it.

These technical meditation instructions are all about facilitating communion, and then union, with the Divine. It is up to you to test them out and determine how useful they are for your spiritual practice. Truly speaking, no spiritual practice, in and of itself, is holy or sacred. The only "Thing" holy or sacred is the Holy One Himself (including His Holy Spirit, the *Sambhogakaya*). Therefore, whatever practices bring you into communion with the Holy One (Samantabhadra, or the Adi Buddha) are the ones you should employ.

Questions and Answers

How would you compare Christian contemplation to Dzogchen?

Mystical, or Eucharistic, Christian contemplation is essentially the same practice as Dzogchen. Holy Communion, understood as the discipline of connecting to Spirit, equates to *trekcho*, and channeling the Holy Spirit mirrors *togal*. In the case of both practices, the goal is a state of infused contemplation, wherein one consciously communes with, and then unites with, the Spirit, or *Sambhogakaya*.

But Dzogchen is about the Great Perfection, which is already the case prior to any attempt to attain Union. Hence, true Dzogchen practice is simply effortlessness.

There has never been, and never will be, a yogi who practiced/practices just "effortlessness" as the means to Enlightenment. The greatest Realizers, including Buddha, Ramana Maharshi, and Milarepa, all had to practice forms of conscious focusing in addition to utter letting go. And even utter letting go doesn't amount to effortlessness, because one has to exert an effort to remain alert in order to remind oneself to resume "declutching" as soon one notices oneself grasping. Prior to full Enlightenment, meaning permanent union with Light-Energy, or Spirit, conscious effortlessness for protracted periods of time is not possible.

But in Tilopa's Song of Mahamudra, *he "sings" that "without making an effort, but remaining loose and natural, one can break the yoke, thus gaining liberation." And Longchen Rabjam, in his teachings, repeatedly enjoins yogis to practice effortlessness.*

Both Tilopa and Naropa, whom Tilopa is addressing in his *Song of Mahamudra*, practiced Anuttarayoga Tantra, a set of spiritual practices intended to accelerate the process of attaining Buddhahood. And Naropa taught his Six Yogas of Naropa rather than just effortlessness, because he knew that effortlessness alone does not cut it as a *sadhana*. But my heretical take is that neither Tilopa nor Naropa understood what "Mahamudra" really means, which is "Great Gesture." "Maha" means "Great" and "Mudra" mean "Gesture"—and this "Great Gesture" is the "Sacrament" (or Sacred Enactment) of Holy Communion, or Yogic At-One-Ment. In other words, the essence of Mahamudra is not effortlessness, but the practice of what I call Plugged-in Presence. This practice generates maximal consciousness-force (or "voltage"), and if it is understood as a synonym for Mahamudra, then there is no need to supplement low-energy, or "effortless," Mahamudra with tantric practices. Rather, "effortlessness," or utter letting go (or "ohms reduction"), becomes the "yin" complement to the "yang" practice (or "Gesture," or "Enactment") of Yogic At-One-Ment, or Plugged-in Presence.

In his Yogic Commentary in the classic W.Y. Evans-Wentz text *Tibetan Yoga and Secret Doctrines*, Translator-Professor Chen-Chi Chang writes: "The Six *Yogas* are productive of more *yogic* power than *Mahamudra*... Traditionally, the *Mahamudra* has been prescribed as a mild antidote, and the Six *Yogas* as a strong antidote, for Ignorance." In other words, because Tilopa and Naropa failed to properly present Mahamudra as direct, immediate conscious at-one-ment, or plugged-in presence, but instead promoted it as passive letting go and self-emptying, it lost its mojo as a "strong antidote for Ignorance," and thus needed to be supplemented with other practices, such as the Six Yogas.

The ramifications of Tilopa and Naropa's misrepresentation of Mahamudra can be seen in the historical presentations of the teachers that followed them. Because none of these Mahamudra teachers of old (including the iconic Dako Tashi Namgyal) or new (such as Geshe Kelsang Gyatso) grokked/grok the true meaning and practice of Mahamudra, they had to incorporate "voltage" practices to compensate for the perceived lack of "yogic power" in Mahamudra.

Because effortlessness, or non-meditation, alone is insufficient as a *sadhana*, Mahamudra developed into a four-phase practice: one-pointedness, simplicity, one taste, and non-meditation. From an "electrical-spiritual" perspective, one-pointedness is a match for voltage, and non-meditation for (maximal) ohm's reduction. Simplicity (non-judging) and one taste (seeing all phenomena as empty) are "in-between" practices that involve degrees of one-pointedness (or focused attention) and non-meditation (or effortlessness).

In his *Song of Mahamudra*, Tilopa describes the yogi's En-Light-ened mind thus: "In the end, it is a great vast ocean, where the Lights of Son and Mother merge in one." The Mother Light—really Mother Light-Energy, or *Sambhogakaya*—is the Spirit-current (amperage). So, from an "electrical-spiritual" perspective, one-pointedness (voltage) is the thesis, non-meditation (ohms reduction) is the antithesis, and the Mother Light-Energy, which subsumes the Son Light (the yogi's consciousness), is the synthesis, which "produces" En-Light-enment, realization of the *Dharmakaya*.

Longchen Rabjam contradicts himself on effortlessness. In *The Precious Treasury of the Way of Abiding* and *A Treasure Trove of Scriptural Transmission: A Commentary on The Precious Treasury of the Basic Space of Phenomena*, he's a salesman for *trekcho* and effortlessness, but in *Precious Treasury of the Genuine Meaning*, he emphasizes the shortcomings of (what he considers) the effortless practice of *trekcho*, and instead promotes the superiority of the effortful practices of *togal*. If he'd known of my Electrical Spiritual Paradigm (ESP), he'd have understood how, in a Dzogchen context, to resolve the effortlessness/effort dialectic by providing the spiritual synthesis that integrates it.

CHAPTER EIGHT

Christian Dzogchen: The Mystical Eucharist

Parallels Between Dzogchen and Christian Mysticism

You've likened Dzogchen to the mystical Eucharist. Can you expand upon their similarities?

I contend that the mystical Eucharist, the sacrament of Holy Communion, mirrors Dzogchen. I see *trekcho* as akin to a Christian mystic's practice of direct presence, whereby he attempts to break through to the "Other Side," the Holy Spirit. And when he breaks through and begins to conduct the Holy Spirit, the Light-Energy continuum, that is the same practice as *togal*. Moreover, as I pointed out in our *togal* discussion, the Four Visions of *Togal* are a ringer for the four stages of en-Light-enment in Christian mysticism: Baptism, Confirmation, Sanctifying Grace, and Divine Union.

The Dzogchen *Trikaya* also mirrors the Christian Trinity. The *Dharmakaya* is the "Father," meaning the Supreme Source, or Divine Being, personified as Samantabhadra, or Adi Buddha. The *Sambhogakaya* is the Holy Spirit, Blessing/Blissing Clear-

Light Energy. And the *Nirmanakaya* is the Son, or Christ, the immanent, or embodied, *Dharmakaya*, or Father.

The parallels between Christianity/Catholicism and Dzogchen/Tibetan Buddhism don't end with the Eucharist/Dzogchen and the Trinity/*Trikaya* correlations, but extend into other areas as well. For example, Tibetan lamas often emphasize their role as a "spiritual friend" to whom their students should openly confess their sins and problems, just as one does with a priest. The Dalai Lama is the Tibetan Buddhist equivalent of the Catholic Pope, and Tibet, until its takeover by the Chinese in the 1950s, was, like Vatican City, a theocracy. And just as there is water baptism in Christianity, there is also a formal ceremony of initiation, or empowerment, by water in Tibetan Buddhism—*wang* (Skt. *abhisheka*), which is anointment by sprinkling. According to Dzongsar Khyentse Rinpoche, *abhisheka* can be translated into Tibetan as *lugpa*, which means "pouring"—as in "pouring blessings."

You've compared Meister Eckhart to Longchen Rabjam to emphasize the similarities between these two mystics. Can you expand upon this?

Both of these iconic mystics, perhaps more than coincidentally, lived in the fourteenth century and taught similar Dharmas, which parallel my Electrical Spiritual Paradigm.

In his wonderful text *The Mystical Thought of Meister Eckhart*, author Bernard McGinn identifies three spiritual processes that represent the core of Eckhart's sermons: breaking through, detaching, and birthing. Breaking through is analogous to plugging

CHAPTER EIGHT: CHRISTIAN DZOGCHEN: THE MYSTICAL EUCHARIST

in (and thereby penetrating to the "Other Side"), detaching is akin to poverty (letting go), and birthing is the process of becoming Christ-like via the Power of Now, the Holy Spirit. The Electrical Spiritual Paradigm is implicit in Eckhart's teachings, and if he were alive and preaching today, he might make the connection between his three core processes and Ohm's Law.

When, several years ago, I first read *The Precious Treasury of the Way of Abiding* by the Tibetan master Longchen Rabjam, I was so excited I nearly fell off my chair. Rabjam's book was a discourse on the four cardinal themes of Dzogchen—spontaneous presence, oneness, openness, and ineffability—that virtually mirrored my still nascent Electrical Spiritual Paradigm. Spontaneous (or direct and immediate) presence plus oneness equaled plugged-in presence (or voltage); openness equated with *poverty* (or ohms reduction); and ineffability referred to the unspeakable, indefinable nature of all phenomena, including the "dynamic energy" (Rabjam's term), or *power* (or amperage), that naturally accompanies awakened awareness or presence. Moreover, in the other Rabjam text I was simultaneously reading, *A Treasure Trove of Scriptural Transmission: A Commentary on The Precious Treasury of the Basic Space of Phenomena*, he described the *togal* practice as relaxing in "the continuum of radiance," which is akin to resting in the Spirit and receiving, or channeling, its Light-Energy. *Togal* is one of the two fundamental meditation practices in Dzogchen; the other is *trekcho*, the practice of breaking through one's resistance to get to the continuum of radiance (the "Other Side"). These two practices are also the foundational ones of Eucharistic, or Electrical, spirituality. In other words, Rabjam's Dzogchen = Eckhart's Christian mysticism = the Plugged-in Presence method (which in its "awakened" form includes channeling Grace, the continuum of Divine radiance).

Can you talk about the Three Sacred Vows of a Christian monk from a Dzogchen perspective?

The Three Sacred Vows—Obedience, Poverty, and Chastity—fit right in with Dzogchen. Obedience is an analogue for *trekcho*, Poverty equals effortlessness, and Chastity equates to *togal*.

Obedience means not avoiding the discipline or practice that connects (or attempts to connect) one to the Holy Spirit, or *Sambhogakaya*. It means devotedly practicing Holy Communion, or *trekcho*.

Poverty means being self-empty, letting go of all effort or resistance. When a mystic is directly present, his presence generates a pressure, or force, that wants to move, and the proper response for him is to yield to it, to let go and let flow. Presence and poverty are a dialectic, with presence being the thesis and poverty the antithesis. And the synthesis is Power, meaning the Holy Spirit, or *Sambhogakaya*, the chaste, or pure, Clear-Light continuum.

Chastity is a synonym for the virgin Spirit, the stainless Clear-Light continuum. It is by converging with the Blessing/Blissing Clear-Light continuum that a yogi becomes en-Light-ened. The "enlightened intent" of Dzogchen is tantamount to the "consent to be Blessed" of Christian mystics. True *togal* (not the "counterfeit" *togal* that became canonical through the Instruction Series) is simply consenting to be Blessed, Blissed, and En-Lightened by the virgin Spirit, the chaste Clear-Light continuum.

CHAPTER NINE

Daist Dzogchen: Radical Understanding

Modern Spiritual Teachings Akin to Dzogchen

Can you identify any modern spiritual teachings, other than your own, that are akin to Dzogchen?

Yes, J. Krishnamurti's and Adi Da's. Krishnamurti's contemplation instructions are incomplete and undeveloped, so his teachings don't merit an in-depth comparison with Dzogchen's. But Da's teachings are a great match for Dzogchen's and provide unique contemplation insights that Dzogchen practitioners should appreciate.

Da's early teachings (written under his birth name of Franklin Jones) are all about what he calls "understanding," which is an analogue for *rigpa*, often described as "radical gnosis." His early teachings, most comprehensively elaborated in his first two books, *The Knee of Listening* and *The Method of the Siddhas* (both written in the early 1970s), describe the Way to Awakening in terms that complement Dzogchen's. Here is an excerpt from *The Knee of Listening* that sounds just like a *rigpa* teaching:

> Understanding is simply to be present, whatever arises, whatever the conditions of cognition or experience, in any world or form. It is to be in relationship, actively, consciously, without implication, prior to the forms of identification, differentiation, and desire that are the products of avoidance. It is to live as the Heart or real action in the midst of these forms, directly consciously, in truth, as enjoyment, in the humor of reality. One who is thus present is the Heart, and he knows it.

Da was a spiritual genius, and if he had trained in the Dzogchen tradition, he'd be revered as one of the tradition's greatest masters. For me, the enquiry he taught, "Avoiding relationship?" (elaborated in *The Knee of Listening* and *The Method of the Siddhas*), has been an invaluable spiritual aid. When I employ it, it spontaneously instigates my return to the *asana* of direct, immediate presence, or relationship. In short, *marigpa* (ignorance) is the avoidance of relationship, and *rigpa* (understanding) is relationship, which, when unqualified, spontaneously morphs into nondual Being-Awareness, or *Dharmata*.

The Heart, or Self, is a synonym for Buddha, or Buddha-nature, and rather than being an exclusive-reductive attempt to realize the Heart, or Self, apart from conditional existence, understanding, in its mature phase, is the action of, rather than the search for, the Heart, or Self. Da writes:

> Understanding is a matter of remaining intelligently present under all conditions, whatever conditions arise, in the enquiry that is in the form of understanding. It is not a mo-

tivated concentration on the Heart or the Self. It is not any inward turning, excluding what has already arisen in consciousness, toward any subtlety or subtler body. It is always enquiry in relationship to whatever arises as cognition and experience at each moment. It is the action of the present Heart, the living Self, not any search for him. It is only knowledge of the exact nature of experience in this instant.

Real meditation, which is a synonym for understanding (or *rigpa*), is, as Da makes clear, a radical (or gone-to-the-root) activity; and it culminates in *Sahaja Samadhi*, continual realization of one's True State *(Dharmata)*. Da writes:

> Real meditation doesn't do anything for you. It has no purpose. When a person begins some form of seeking, he immediately turns to an effective, remedial technique that will get him quickly to his goal. But real life, the way of understanding, is not another form of seeking. For the man of understanding, meditation is not adopted for the sake of something else. He does not pursue understanding or reality or any kind of experience through meditation. Real meditation is already a radical activity. It is understanding.
>
> There are various forms of dhyana, or meditation. But perfect, absolute radical understanding is the most intense, the endless or eternal Form of meditation. When this meditation is itself perfect, radical, absolute, when re-cognition has become total, when everything has been re-cognized, so that nothing arises in consciousness that is not at the very same instant already re-cognized, when regardless of the

condition that arises, regardless of the activity that is performed, when one is sitting as if in meditation, or walking, or performing ordinary activity, the Real Form is only obvious, when re-cognition is constant, that is the fundamental state. This is true Samadhi, Sahaja Samadhi, constant realization of one's true state prior to all conditions in the worlds. This true Samadhi or realization is not itself an experience, a kind of trance or any kind of "yogic" state. It is only the enjoyment of and as that Reality which one has always been and which all things are. One who simply enjoys and lives this enjoyment is to be called a "man of understanding."

Dzogchen doesn't acknowledge a Self, so how do you reconcile its teachings with Adi Da's?

Dzogchen "smuggles" in a Self under the guise of the *Nirmanakaya*. The *Nirmanakaya* is the immanent, or indwelling, *Dharmakaya*, which is absolute Awareness, or Consciousness. The Self, per the Hindus, is absolute Consciousness; so, whether one refers to this Body, or Dimension, as Self, or *Nirmanakaya*, or Buddha-nature, the reference is to the same Hypostasis.

Do Adi Da's teachings have an energetic dimension that parallels Dzogchen's?

Da developed and refined his Energy teachings over time, and they provide the most sophisticated descriptions of the en-Light-enment process that I've encountered. That said, in essence, they parallel Dzogchen's, and this will be clear to those who understand that what Da calls "the Shakti" is the same

Body, or Dimension, as the *Sambhogakaya*. Just as Dzogchen *togal* is about contemplating and uniting with the *Sambhogakaya*, or *Shakti*, so are Da's teachings.

Da's description of his Awakening provides a fine example of his view of the role of Energy, or *Shakti*, in the Enlightenment project. The following (redacted) description is from his spiritual autobiography, *The Knee of Listening*:

> Then [in the Vedanta Society Temple] I felt the Divine Shakti appear in Person, Pressed against my own natural body, and, altogether, against my Infinitely Expanded, and even formless, Form. She Embraced me, Openly and Utterly, and we Combined with One Another in Divine (and Motionless, and spontaneously Yogic) "Sexual Union". We Found One Another Thus, in a Fire of most perfect Desire, and for no other Purpose than This Union, and, yet, as if to Give Birth to the universes. In That most perfect Union, I Knew the Oneness of the Divine Energy and my Very Being. There was no separation at all, nor had there ever been, nor would there ever be. The One Being that Is my own Ultimate Self-Nature was revealed most perfectly. The One Being Who I Am was revealed to Include the Reality that Is Consciousness Itself, the Reality that Is the Source-Energy of all conditional appearances, and the Reality that Is all conditional manifestation, All as a Single Force of Being, an Eternal Union, and an Irreducible cosmic Unity.
>
> The next day, September 10, 1970, I sat in the [Vedanta Society] temple again. I awaited the Beloved Shakti to re-

veal Herself in Person, as my Blessed Companion. But, as time passed, there was no Event of changes, no movement at all. There was not even any kind of inward deepening, no "inwardness" at all. There was no meditation. There was no need for meditation. There was not a single element or change that could be added to make my State Complete. I sat with my eyes open. I was not having an experience of any kind. Then, suddenly, I understood most perfectly. I Realized that I had Realized. The "Thing" about the "Bright" became Obvious. I Am Complete. I Am the One Who Is Complete.

In That instant, I understood and Realized (inherently, and most perfectly) What and Who I Am. It was a tacit Realization, a direct Knowledge in Consciousness. It was Consciousness Itself, without the addition of a Communication from any "Other" Source. There Is no "Other" Source. I simply sat there and Knew What and Who I Am. I was Being What I Am, Who I Am. I Am Being What I Am, Who I Am. I Am Reality, the Divine Self, the Nature, Substance, Support, and Source of all things and all beings. I Am the One Being, called "God" (the Source and Substance and Support and Self of all), the "One Mind" (the Consciousness and Energy in and As Which all appears), "Siva-Shakti" (the Self-Existing and Self-Radiant Reality Itself), "Brahman" (the Only Reality, Itself), the "One Atman" (That Is not ego, but Only "Brahman", the Only Reality, Itself), the "Nirvanic Ground" (the egoless and conditionless Reality and Truth, Prior to all dualities, but excluding none). I Am the One and Only and necessarily Divine Self, Nature, Condition, Substance, Support, Source, and Ground of all. I Am the "Bright."

Later I described that most perfect Realization as follows:

At the Vedanta Society Temple inherent and most perfect Knowledge arose that I Am simply the "Bright" Consciousness that Is Reality. The traditions call It the "Self", "Brahman", "Shiva-Shakti", and so many other names. It is identified with no body, no functional sheath, no conditional realm, and no conditional experience, but It is the inherently perfect, unqualified, Absolute Reality. I saw that there is nothing to which this Ultimate Self-Nature can be compared, or from which It can be differentiated, or by which It can be epitomized. It does not stand out. It is not the equivalent of any specialized, exclusive, or separate Spiritual state. It cannot be accomplished, acquired, discovered, remembered, or perfected—since It is inherently perfect, and It is always already the case.

So, what Da calls the "Bright Consciousness" represents the union of Siva *and* Shakti *(or* Siva-Shakti*), which equates to the union of the* Dharmakaya *and the* Sambhogakaya *(or* Dharmakaya-Sambhogakaya*)?*

Yes. *Siva* and the *Dharmakaya* are Consciousness Itself, while *Shakti* and the *Sambhogakaya* are Bright, or Clear-Light, Energy. And the union of these two Dimensions of Reality "produces," or unveils, "Bright Consciousness." This union occurs in the spiritual Heart-center (*Hridayam,* or *Tathagatagarbha*), the seat of the soul, or human consciousness, which Buddhists call *citta*. The Bright Light of *Shakti,* the *Sambhogakaya,* illuminates and awakens *citta,* engendering the State (or non-state) of *Bodhicitta.* It could be said that *citta* is the contracted *Nirmanakaya* and that *Bodhicitta* is the de-contracted *Nirmanakaya*.

But later in The Knee of Listening, *Da writes, "At last I saw it was not a matter of Shakti experiences, or even Self-experiences, but of understanding as a radical path or premise."*

There are two fundamental ways to view En-Light-enment: as the union of one's consciousness (or soul) with Light-Energy (or *Shakti*), or as radical Be-ing, meaning being directly present as Consciousness and gnostically obviating obstructions to this Presence. Notice that Da's description of his (Vedanta Temple) Awakening is about the former, uniting with the *Shakti*, while his post-Awakening teachings emphasize the latter, just being present and understanding (and hence undermining) impediments to immediate nondual Be-ing. But the fact of the matter is that even if one adopts this radical nondual spiritual approach, the "mechanics" of En-Light-enment dictate that one's consciousness must unite with *Shakti* in the Heart-center for Self-realization, or Buddhahood, to occur.

So, you reject the Zen view that there is just the Dharmakaya, *that the idea of the* Trikaya *is superfluous?*

Yes. While I certainly appreciate Zen Master Huang Po's teachings, such as "There's never been a single thing. If you can understand the heart of this, why talk of transcendental bliss [meaning the *Sambhogakaya*]?" I don't second the Zen rejection of the *Trikaya*. In accordance with Dzogchen, I advocate a *Trikayan* (or Trinitarian) view of En-Light-enment because it more fully explains the Awakening project. Moreover, I also advocate the practice of *togal*, which Zen fails to acknowledge, though it is implicit in its Mind-awakening practices. But, as made clear in our discussions, my views on *togal* and the *Trikaya* are contrary to those of traditional Dzogchen.

CHAPTER TEN

Dzogchen Discursion

Open-ended Dzogchen Discussion

In this discussion, instead of focusing on a specific topic, we'll freely consider anything pertaining to Dzogchen. Because our discussion will move to and fro, we'll call it "Dzogchen Discursion." So, go ahead with your questions and comments.

Can you clarify the definitions of Dharma, Dharmakaya, Dharmadhatu, Dharmamegha, *and* Dharmata?

Dharma, when capitalized, means the True Condition of a thing. When not capitalized, *dharma* means a thing or existent. *Dharma*, when capitalized, is also a synonym for Truth Teaching. Hence, the *Dharma*, or Doctrine, taught by Gautama was about realizing the True Condition of Reality, *Nirvana*.

The *Dharmakaya* is the Truth, or Reality, "Body," or Dimension. It is timeless Awareness, or Mind, the ineffable Self-Existing, Self-Conscious "Substance" underlying and transcending all *dharmas*, or things. When the *Dharmakaya* is referred to as the "basic space of phenomena," it is called the *Dharmadhatu*. But Dzogchen errs when it conflates the *Dharmadhatu* with space; for, in reality, the "space" in which phenomena arise is spaceless as well as timeless. Hence, *Dharmadhatu* is simply the term for the *Dharmakaya* as spaceless Awareness, the universal Context of all content, or phenomena.

If the Dharmadhatu *is spaceless, what is space?*

Space is the *Akasha*, the ether. Whereas the *Dharmakaya/Dharmadhatu* is uncreated, prior to and outside time and space, the ether, universal space, is created, and, along with time, it began in conjunction with the universe.

Dharmamegha is the *Dharmakaya* in its "phase" or "form" as "Grace," Blessing Power poured down on *bodhisattvas*. It is the "raineddown" descent of the *Dharmakaya* (as the *Sambhogakaya*), which, when "full-blown," "produces" *Bodhicitta*. Sometimes, the term "Great *Dharmamegha*" is used to differentiate "full" *Dharmamegha* from "partial" *Dharmamegha*, meaning *Shaktipat* insufficient to yield Buddhahood. Great *Dharmamegha* is the "Dharma Cloud" bursting and showering a *bodhisattva* with sufficient *Shaktipat* to yield *Bodhicitta*. It is the unobstructed *Sambhogakaya* uniting with the *Nirmanakaya* in the Heart-cave, or *Tathagatagarbha*, so as to "produce" *Dharmata*, the realization of Mind-as-Thusness, or Being-Consciousness.

What can you say about Guru yoga, which is so highly esteemed in Dzogchen?

Guru yoga means union with the True Nature of a Guru, which is Clear Light, which removes one's darkness, or ignorance. Hence, it is the epitome of yoga and Dzogchen. In Dzogchen, there are three levels of the Guru—outer, inner, and secret. The outer Guru can be a historical figure, such as Gautama or Longchen Rabjam, but usually it is one's living, physically present Guru. The inner Guru is one's *yidam*, or personal meditation deity. And the secret Guru is one's own Buddha-nature, or True Self.

A living, physical Guru, or Buddha, spontaneously, ceaselessly emits radiant Light-Energy; so when a mature disciple communes with his spiritual Transmission, his mirror-like Presence, he can apperceive his own Buddha-nature. A *yidam*, or personal meditation deity, can also serve as a doorway to the recognition of one's Buddha-nature, for when, in the act of communion with the image of the deity, the image falls away, one's Buddha-nature stands out. A gifted disciple has no need of an outer or inner Guru, for he is able to directly recognize, and even radiate as, the secret Guru, his own Buddha-nature.

What can you say about the Kayas *apart from the* Trikaya?

First, there is the *Rupakaya*, the form body of an Enlightened being. It is a "product" of the union of the *Sambhogakaya* and the *Nirmanakaya* in the Heart-center. Then there is the so-called Fourth Body, the *Svabhavakaya*, described as the union or non-separation of the three *Kayas* of the *Trikaya*. Because it just describes the unified State of the *Trikaya* after Enlightenment, it isn't a distinct Body per se. Beyond the Fourth Body is a Fifth Body, the *Mahasukhakaya*, the "Great Bliss Body," which likewise is not a distinct Body, but merely the State of the *Sambhogakaya* post-Enlightenment. Still another non-distinct Body that describes the post-Enlightenment *Sambhogakaya* is the *Vajrakaya*, which means "Indestructible Body" of full Enlightenment.

And, most famously, there is the Rainbow Body, typically described as a Body of Pure Light accompanied by lights and rainbows. It is usually associated with the death experience and the dematerialization of the physical body, but exceptional yogis are said to be able to experience it without dying. The Rainbow Body, like the *Mahasukhakaya* and the *Vajrakaya*, is not a distinct Body, but yet another description of the post-Enlightenment *Sambhogakaya*. The *Sambhogakaya* itself is the Body of Pure, or Clear, Light, and when it is affixed to a human form body, that body, like a prism, can refract the Clear Light into colors and rainbows.

Do you agree with the commonly held Dzogchen view that "the fundamental point of practice is to distinguish rigpa from sems (citta, (grasping) mind)"?

No. First off, *citta*, when unimplicated by *manas* or *vijnana*, is not the grasping mind; it is consciousness itself. And when it is freed as *Bodhicitta*, it shines as *Cit*, transcendental Consciousness, or Mind. *Citta*, unlike *manas* and *vijnana*, is not a *prakritic* or *samsaric* evolute (meaning a created constituent principle).

Secondly, the fundamental point of Dzogchen practice, or *rigpa*, is to be Mind, or conscious Presence, not to seek to distinguish it from the grasping mind (*manas* functioning as *vijnana*). When one is present as Mind, the distinction between pure, or thought-free, Mind and impure, or grasping, mind is Self-evident. Hence, distinguishing Mind from mind is a secondary and spontaneous function of Dzogchen practice.

What can you say about the transmission of Mind from a Guru to a disciple?

Mind (the "Subjective" Dimension of Reality) can never be cognized as an object; hence it cannot be directly transmitted. Only Clear-Light Energy (the "Objective" Dimension of Reality) can be directly transmitted, and in the Bright "Mirror" of Clear Light, provided through the medium of a Guru, the astute disciple can apperceive his Self (or Buddha)-Nature as Mind.

What about the various transmissions and levels of transmissions?

They are about degrees of intensity, degrees of *Shaktipat* that the disciple receives. The more intense the Spirit-current, the brighter shines the concomitant "Mirror" of Clear Light.

More specifically, there are Four Empowerments, or levels of *abhisheka* (Pouring of the Blessing), in Dzogchen: *Nirmanakaya*, *Sambhogakaya*, *Dharmakaya*, and *Svabhavakaya*. The *Nirmanakaya* level corresponds with Spirit-baptism received through the form body, the *Sambhogakaya* with repeated Confirmation and sustained contemplation of the Spirit, the *Dharmakaya* with awakening to Buddha as Mind, and the *Svabhavakaya* with realizing the union or non-separation of the *Kayas*.

The Four Empowerments sound just like the Four Visions of Togal.

Yes, and they likewise correspond with the four mystical Christian sacraments of Baptism, Confirmation, Sanctuary (or Sanctifying Grace), and Divine Union.

What do you see for the future of Dzogchen?

Further refinement of its Dharma in the context of the Esoteric Perennial Philosophy, which elaborates En-Light-enment through the lens of trinitarianism. This especially pertains to *togal* teachings, which, in their current form, represent the perversion of the Great Perfection. Longchen Rabjam's *Precious Treasury of the Genuine Meaning* and Jigme Lingpa's *Yeshe Lama* need to be scrapped, and supplanted by proper *togal* teachings, presented in the context of esoteric trinitarianism.

Trekcho teachings also need to be upgraded. Not only are they improperly presented as "effortless," in contrast to the "effort" required in *togal*, but they are also incompletely explained. If Dzogchen adopted my Electrical Spiritual Paradigm, *trekcko* would be elucidated as a dialectic with presence/relationship as the thesis (voltage), letting go/self-emptying as the antithesis (ohms reduction), and the Spirit-current/*Sambhogakaya* as the synthesis (amperage). This synthesis would seamlessly slide *trekcho* into *togal*, and explain how the consciousness-force generated by *trekcho* translates into *togal*, conductivity of the flow of the Spirit-current/*Sambhogakaya*, the Light-Energy continuum that "produces" En-Light-enment.

CHAPTER ELEVEN

Dzogchen Literature: A Cognizant Overview

Recommended Spiritual Texts

What books do you recommend for those looking to deepen and widen their understanding of Dzogchen?

My nonfiction books provide an extensive Spiritual Reading List that includes a Dzogchen category of Highly Recommended and Recommended texts. [See the back of this book for the List.] But to more deeply understand Dzogchen, I think it's also important to read spiritual books outside the Tibetan ambit. Let's first consider those before we turn to the Dzogchen texts.

I'll start with J. Krishnamurti (1895-1986), a spiritual iconoclast who rejected association with any tradition. His "Dharma," if we can call it that, was entirely self-originated and reflects profound insight into the Awakening project. The essence of the contemplation practice he advocated is effortless, choiceless awareness, which accords with Dzogchen. Although he doesn't adequately expand upon this practice and delve into the esoteric or energetic aspects of en-Light-enment, the deep psychological insights he provides make him a worthwhile read. I strongly suggest his *First and Last Freedom*, and if that floats your boat, then get *Commentaries on Living*, which is more of the same, presented in the context of meetings with his students.

I've already elaborated the similarity between Adi Da's radical understanding teachings and Dzogchen in a previous discussion. Again, the two Da books I most highly recommend are *The Knee of Listening* and *The Method of the Siddhas*. I suggest early (used) editions of these books (written under one of Da's first two names, Franklin Jones or Bubba Free John), because they most deeply detail radical understanding.

The highest teachings in Tibetan Buddhism are Dzogchen (Atiyoga) and Mahamudra, which are similar. Both of these teachings emphasize the practice of being directly aware, or present, and not seeking for anything. In *Teachings of Tibetan Yoga*, author Garma C.C. Chang's translation of *The Song of Mahamudra* by Tilopa is absolutely elegant. No other Mahamudra presentation I've read matches its poetic quality. And I'm not the only mystic to think this. The late Osho (Bhagwan Shree Rajneesh) chose Chang's translation for his elaboration of Mahamudra in his book *Only One Sky*. In addition to *The Song of Mahamudra*, Chang also provides a supplementary section on Mahamudra—*The Essentials of Mahamudra Practice* by Lama Kong Ka—that is, in a word, superb. Lama Kong Ka provides all kinds of useful insights and information on the practice of Mahamudra that I haven't found in any other Tibetan Buddhist text. On top of the unmatched Mahamudra descriptions, this book also includes an outstanding presentation of the Six Yogas of Naropa.

Another fine Tibetan Yoga text I recommend is W.Y. Evans-Wentz's classic *Tibetan Yoga and Secret Doctrines,* which also provides descriptions of Mahamudra and the Six Yoga of Naropa. Some of the later editions of this book no longer include the Preface to the second edition Yogic Commentary by Translator-Professor Chen-Chi Chang. Be sure to get an edition that includes it. Professor Chen-Chi Chang is none other than Garma C.C. Chang, who authored *Teachings of Tibetan Yoga* as well as *The Hundred Thousand Songs of Milarepa*. Professor Chang, an expert in Zen as well as Tibetan Buddhism, offers some very insightful observations about Mahamudra (as classically taught) versus Zen meditation. In agreement with me, he views Mahamudra as a low-energy spiritual practice. If he were still alive, I'm sure he'd appreciate my Electrical Spiritual Paradigm, which explains why it is low energy. Because Mahamudra is low energy, the legendary Naropa also taught, as a supplementary practice, the Yoga of the Six Doctrines—the Doctrines of the Psychic-Heat, the Illusory Body, the Dream-State, the Clear Light, the After-Death State, and the Consciousness-Transference. And this book, like Chang's *Teachings of Tibetan Yoga*, details the practices of these yogas.

Chogyam Trungpa's classic *Cutting Through Spiritual Materialism* is a worthwhile read for beginner-to-intermediate Dharma practitioners. It's well-written, entertaining, and exposes the many pitfalls on the spiritual path. But if you're interested in deep, demystifying Tibetan Buddhism, you won't find it in this text.

Now, let's turn to the Dzogchen texts. I don't claim to have read every Dzogchen text, but I've read extensively enough to have a good overview of the genre. And I believe that anyone who reads all the Dzogchen texts I recommend will gain a more than sufficient understanding of the tradition and practice. I've reviewed most of the Dzogchen texts on my Spiritual Reading List (and plenty more) at my blog electricalspirituality.com, so anyone who wants more information on the books I recommend (and those I don't) should check out my reviews. And my Kindle book *Buddhist Book Reviews for Smarties*, available at Amazon, contains not only all my reviews of Dzogchen books, but all my reviews of Buddhist books.

The best Dzogchen meditation text I've encountered is Namkhai Norbu's *The Cycle of Day and Night: An Essential Tibetan Text on the Practice of Contemplation*. Although I've been critical of Norbu in my talks, until he passed, in 2018, he was probably the foremost living Dzogchen teacher, and is must-reading for those into Dzogchen. This is his best book, not only because of the content, but because it's edited by John Myrdhin Reynolds, an outstanding Dzogchen scholar. And a great complementary text to Norbu's *The Cycle of Day and Night* is Reynold's *The Golden Letters*, a tome that elaborates Dzogchen essentials and history in the context of the Three Statements of Garab Dorje, the so-called "first teacher of Dzogchen."

Longchen Rabjam, revered as one of the greatest Dzogchen masters and scholar-writers, is essential reading for all Dzogchen students. And the best presentation and translation of his writings can be found in the Seven Treasury Series by Padma Publishing. I recommend starting with *The Precious Treasury of Abiding*, and then moving on to *A Treasure Trove of Scriptural Transmission: A Commentary on The Precious Treasury of the Basic Space of Phenomena*. These wonderful texts are a pleasure to read and a veritable fountain of Dharma wisdom.

Another Rabjam text worth checking out is *The Practice of Dzogchen*, an anthology of Longchen Rabjam's writings on Dzogchen by Longchen Rabjam and Tulku Thondup. This massive tome is probably the largest collection of Rabjam's writings in a single volume, but the translation and writing in my 2002 edition are substandard, which is why I didn't include it on my Spiritual Reading List. However, a new edition, which I haven't checked out, was published in 2014, and hopefully it's an improvement over the 2002 edition.

Although, as I make clear in our discussions on *togal*, I have nothing good to say about Rabjam's *Precious Treasury of the Genuine Meaning*, it's also must-reading for those interested in standard *togal*, as is Jigme Lingpa's *Yeshe Lama*, another text I hold in low regard. Sam van Schaik's *Approaching the Great Perfection: Simultaneous and Gradual Methods of Dzogchen Practice in the Longchen Nyingtig* and *Naked Seeing: The Great Perfection, the Wheel of Time and Visionary Buddhism in Renaissance Tibet* by Christopher Hatchell are both interesting, information-packed academic texts that serious students of *togal* will appreciate.

The *Kunjed Gyalpo*, the fundamental Tantra of Dzogchen Sem-de, is important reading for serious students of Dzogchen, which is why I included *The Supreme Source* (by Namkhai Norbu and Adriano Clemente), a translation and commentary of this Tantra, on my Spiritual Reading List. Another version of *Kunjed Gyalpo*, titled *The All-Creating King* (by Christopher Wilkinson), which I have not read, has recently become available, so this is another option. Yet another option is just reading *A Treasure Trove of Scriptural Transmission: A Commentary on The Precious Treasury of the Basic Space of Phenomena*, which provides insightful commentaries on so many excerpts from the *Kunjed Gyalpo* that non-serious students of Dzogchen can skip on the text itself.

The "Yoga of Knowing the Mind," attributed to the legendary Padmasambhava, is a classic Dzogchen teaching originally rendered into English under the direction of W.Y. Evans-Wentz. Published in 1954 as *The Tibetan Book of the Great Liberation*, it was the standard translation of, and commentary on, this work until John Myrdhin Reynolds' *Self-Liberation: Through Seeing with Naked Awareness* hit the market in 2010. Reynolds, in his book, makes it clear that he holds Evans-Wentz's work in low esteem and considers it deeply flawed. And he devotes considerable space to elaborating its "problems." I don't agree with all of Reynolds' criticisms, and though his translation is no doubt more precise than Evans-Wentz's, I find it flatter and less inspiring. My suggestion is to get both versions and compare them for yourself.

Naked Awareness: Practical Instructions on the Union of Mahamudra and Dzogchen by Karma Chagme is another book I recommend. Translated by B. Alan Wallace, with commentary by his guru, Gyatrul Rinpoche, it is teeming with meaty, esoteric content, though the commentary is less than first rate. In this classic seventeenth-century presentation, Chagme integrates the two great meditation systems of Tibet: Mahamudra and Dzogchen.

Rodney P. Devenish's *Principal Yogacara Texts: Indo-Tibetan Sources of Dzogchen Mahamudra* is chock-full of translations of Dharma texts I haven't encountered elsewhere. And the texts (which Devenish describes as "Yogic Treatises") are wonderful—enlightening and educational, providing the Indic source texts from which Dzogchen stems. Although Devenish's commentary doesn't impress, the texts alone make this book a worthwhile read.

Dzogchen as taught in the Bon tradition is similar to Dzogchen as taught in the Buddhist tradition, yet there are differences worth examining. Among the Bon Dzogchen texts I've read, which aren't that many, the most informative is easily Tenzin Wangyal's *Wonders of the Natural Mind: The Essence of Dzogchen in the Native Bon Tradition of Tibet*. Although I'm critical of Wangyal's explanations of esoteric aspects of Dzogchen, the sheer amount of educative information he provides, along with useful practice advice and instruction, makes this a recommended text.

That's it for my reading suggestions. Are there any questions?

You haven't mentioned Jackson Peterson, Keith Dowman, or Tulku Urgyen Rinpoche. Have you read their books?

Yes, I've read their books and plenty of other Dzogchen texts as well. If I thought they added to my recommended readings, I'd have mentioned them.

Glossary

Abhisheka: The formal ceremony of initiation, or empowerment, by water in Tibetan Buddhism—which is anointment by sprinkling. Per Dzongsar Khyentse Rinpoche, *abhisheka* (Skt.) can be translated into Tibetan as *lugpa*, which means "pouring"—as in "pouring blessings."

Adi Buddha: The primordial *Buddha*, a.k.a. *Samantabhadra*, who is akin to *Siva* in tantric Saivism.

Advaita Vedanta: The nondual school of Hindu philosophy which asserts that one's True Self (*Atman*) is the same as the Divine Being (*Brahman*).

Ajna Chakra: The third-eye *chakra*, and the sixth primary chakra (of seven) in the body, according to Hindu yoga. The Dzogchen tradition, however, does not recognize it as a primary *chakra*. Rather, it identifies just four primary *chakras*: the navel, heart, throat, and crown.

Akasha: The ether, or universal space element, wherefrom the four fundamental elements (fire, earth, air, water) derive.

Alaya: The unborn Realm, universal Mind.

Alaya-vijnana: The *Alaya* (universal Consciousness) conjoined with *manas* by *vijnana* in the Heart-center/cave, the *Tathagatagarbha*. A synonym for *citta*, which functions as the "storehouse consciousness," or repository, of one's psychical seed impressions/tendencies (*samskaras*).

Amrita Nadi: The Force (or *Shakti*)-current between the spiritual Heart-center and the crown. The terminal portion of *sushumna nadi*, through which immortal "Nectar," Blessing/Blissing Clear-Light Energy, flows.

Ananda: Bliss—really *Shakti*-Bliss—which stems from the enactment of Being-Consciousness (*Sat-Cit*).

Anandamaya kosha: The Bliss Sheath (or Body). *Shakti* (the *Sambhogakaya*) perceived and enjoyed as separate from *Siva* (the *Dharmakaya*). In *Vedanta*, the fifth of the five sheaths covering (and thus preventing the realization of) the immanent Self (or *Buddha*).

Ananda-Shakti: Divine Blissing Power. The *Sambhogakaya* as the dynamic Bliss Body.

Annamaya kosha: The sheath composed of food; that is, of material elements: the physical body. In *Vedanta*, the first of the five sheaths covering the Self.

Anugraha-Shakti: Divine Blessing Power, or Grace.

Anuyoga: The tantra vehicle of the Nyingmapa school of Tibetan Buddhism that emphasizes meditation on the inner or subtle body, including *chakras*, *nadis*, and winds.

Arya-bodhisattva: A *bodhisattva* who has directly, though impermanently, realized *Tathata*, or Suchness, or Beingness.

Asana: Psycho-physical "position," "seat," or "stance."

Atiyoga: The highest tantra of the Nyingmapa school of Tibetan Buddhism and a synonym for Dzogchen. Primordial yoga, meaning the yogic enactment of the Great Perfection.

Atman: A synonym for Self, Christ, or *Buddha*. Immanent *Brahman*, or Divine Reality.

Atma Nadi: A synonym for *Amrita Nadi*.

Avadhuti: One of the three principal *nadis* that connect the base of the spine to the crown. As the so-called central channel, it lies between the so-called left channel, *lalana*, and the so-called right channel, *rasana*, each of which coil around it and intersect at points within it, forming the major "spinal" *chakras*. Per Dzogchen, there are four such *chakras*—at the navel, heart, throat, and crown. *Avadhuti* is an analogue for *sushumna* in Hindu yoga.

Bhumi: Stage or level. Typically used in Mahayana Buddhism to describe the ten stages or levels of spiritual attainment that culminate in Buddhahood.

Bindu: A synonym for *thigle* in Dzogchen. A small point, "drop," or sphere (sometimes described as the size of a thumbnail) that is luminous and without discernible edges.

Bodhicitta: Enlightened, or Awakened, Consciousness. *Buddhahood*.

Bodhisattva: An Enlightenment-minded seeker of *Bodhicitta*.

Brahman: Ultimate Reality. The changeless, infinite Divine Being, typically described as *Sat-Cit-Ananda*.

Buddha / Buddha-Nature: A synonym for *Atman*, Self, or Christ. The immanent *Dharmakaya*, or Mind.

Buddhadharma: Buddhist *Dharma*, or Teaching.

Buddhahood: A synonym for *Bodhicitta* and *Nirvana*.

Buddhi: The intellect, or discriminating intelligence of the mind. Sometimes referred to as the "higher mind," in contrast to *manas*, the "lower mind."

Chakra: Literally a "wheel" or "center." The major *chakras* are subtle-body centers where *pranic* channels converge into rotating vortices of energy, which, when blocked, can be likened to "knots," and when open, can produce various "spiritual" phenomena.

Cit: Universal, transcendental Consciousness.

Citta: Immanent Consciousness itself (*Cit*) intertwined with *manas* and contracted by grasping (or acts of binding attention) engendered by *vijnana*. When *citta* is permanently de-contracted, it shines as *Cit*, or *Bodhicitta*, and though functioning as *manas* and *vijnana*, it is no longer contracted by them. This is tantamount to the conversion of the *Alaya-vijnana* from an "organ" of bondage and becoming to an "instrument" of Enlightenment.

Dharma / dharma: When capitalized, spiritual teaching or Truth or Law. When uncapitalized, conditional things.

Dharmadhatu: The *Dharmakaya* as the all-pervading, spaceless Substratum underlying phenomenal existence.

Dharmakaya: Universal, timeless Awareness or Consciousness.

Dharmamegha: The "rained-down" descent of the *Dharmakaya* (as the *Sambhogakaya*) which, when "full-blown," "produces" *Bodhicitta*. Sometimes, the term "Great *Dharmamegha*" is used to differentiate "full-blown" *Dharmamegha* from "partial" *Dharmamegha*.

Dharmata: The *Dharmakaya* as universal Suchness, or Beingness. The True Nature of existence. A synonym for *Tathata*.

Dhyana: Meditation. The Sanskrit equivalent of Japanese *Zen* and Chinese *Chan*.

Dzogchen: The Great Perfection. The Tibetan Buddhist and Bon traditions/practices aimed at directly realizing the primordial State of Being.

Guru: Remover of darkness, or ignorance. A Self-realized being who unobstructedly radiates Light.

Hridaya/Hridayam: The spiritual Heart. A synonym for the immanent Self and the Center, relative to the body, through which it radiates.

Hridaya-granthi: The Heart-knot, which, when severed, results in Self-realization and the "regeneration" of *Amrita Nadi*, which rises from the Heart-center (felt/experienced two digits to the right of center of one's chest) to the Crown, and beyond.

Hridaya-Shakti: The radiant *Shakti* emitted from/through the Heart-center of an Enlightened one. A synonym for the *Nirmanakaya* in standard Dzogchen teachings. [Note: my definition of *Nirmanakaya* does not equate it with *Hridaya-Shakti*.]

Ida: The Hindu yoga analogue for *lalana* (see *lalana*).

Jhana: Meditative state of engrossment. The Four *Jhanas*, which constitute the eighth limb (Right Contemplation) of the Buddha's Noble Eightfold path, are progressive states of engrossment in the Stream, or Spirit-current. In yogic terminology, they equate to *samadhis*.

Jiva: The individual soul or being.

Kadag: One of the two fundamental aspects of *rigpa* (the other being *lhun gub*). It means "primordial purity," and thus is a match for *trekcho*.

Kaya: Body, or hypostasis; mode or dimension of Being.

Kosha: Sheath, or covering.

Kundalini / Kundalini-Shakti: The "serpent power." The dynamic force-flow of "uncoiled" energy that accompanies spiritual awakening. The so-called "higher *Kundalini*" refers to *Shaktipat*, the descent of Divine Power.

Lalana: One of the three principal *nadis* that connect the base of the spine to the crown. The so-called left channel, it coils around the central channel, *avudhati*, and at the points within the central channel where it intersects the so-called right channel, *rasana*, the major "spinal" *chakras* are formed. Per Dzogchen, there are four such *chakras*—at the navel, heart, throat, and crown. *Lalana* is an analogue for *ida* in Hindu yoga.

Lhun Grub: One of the two fundamental aspects of *rigpa* (the other being *kadag*). It means "spontaneous presence," and thus is a match for *togal*.

Lugpa: "Pouring"—as in "pouring blessings."

Madhyamaka: A school of Mahayana Buddhism, systematized by Nagarjuna, which emphasizes the emptiness of all phenomena.

Mahamudra: The Great Seal, Symbol, and Gesture. And the "Great Gesture," or yogic "Holo-Act," is uniting the son light (the *nirmanakaya*) with the Mother Light (the *Sambhogakaya*), which yields realization of the *Dharmakaya*.

Mahasukhakaya: Beyond the so-called Fourth Body (see *Svabhavakaya*) is a so-called Fifth Body, the *Mahasukhakaya*, the "Great Bliss Body," which likewise is not a distinct Body, but the State of the *Sambhogakaya* post-Enlightenment.

Mahayoga: The tantra yoga vehicle of the Nyingmapa school of Tibetan Buddhism that emphasizes visualization.

Manas: The mind that processes and mediates sensory information and habit-tendencies (*vasanas*). The mind in general, sometimes referred to as the "lower mind," in contrast to the *buddhi*, the "higher mind."

Manomaya kosha: The sheath of mind. In *Vedanta*, the third of the five sheaths covering the Self.

Marigpa: Spiritual ignorance and the absence of presence. The antipode of *rigpa*, which is spiritual gnosis and presence.

Maya: That which has been measured out from the Immeasurable; phenomenal existence or reality.

Nadis: Energy channels in the body. These include the subtle-body channels through which *prana* and *Kundalini* flow and, in the case of *Amrita Nadi*, the causal-body channel through which immortal "Nectar," Blessing/Blissing Clear-Light Energy, streams.

Nirmanakaya: The immanent *Dharmakaya*. The Enlightened form body, or manifest *Buddha*; akin to the Christian Son, or Christ.

Nirvana: The end of becoming (*samsara*), which signifies Blissful Divine Being. Equivalent to Hindu *Sat-Cit-Ananda*.

Pingala: The Hindu yoga analogue for *rasana* (see *rasana*).

Prajna: Transcendental wisdom or understanding.

Prakriti: The primal "matter" or substance from which the physical and mental universe evolves. Whatever is created is *prakritic* in nature, meaning finite, conditioned, and temporary.

Prana: Etheric life-force energy; equivalent to *chi*.

Prana-shakti: The palpable, intensified flow of etheric life-force energy.

Pranayama: Conscious breathing exercise(s) aimed at balancing and/or intensifying the flow of *prana* through one's *nadis*.

Pranamaya kosha: The sheath composed of life-force: the etheric body in Western occult literature. In *Vedanta*, the second of five sheaths covering the Self.

Rasana: One of the three principal *nadis* that connect the base of the spine to the crown. The so-called right channel, it coils around the central channel, *avudhati*, and at the points within the central channel where it intersects the so-called left channel, *lalana,* the major "spinal" *chakras* are formed. Per Dzogchen, there are four such *chakras*—at the navel, heart, throat, and crown. *Lalana* is an analogue for *pingala* in Hindu yoga.

Rigpa: The fundamental Dzogchen practice of direct, immediate presence, which fosters radical (or gone-to-the root) spiritual gnosis. *Rigpa* consists of the two sub-practices of *trekcho* and *togal*, which, in combination, "produce," or unveil, the progressive recognition, manifestation, and realization of *Dharmata*.

Rupakaya: The form body of an Enlightened being.

Sadhana: Spiritual practice.

Sahaja Samadhi: The "State" (or non-state) of unbroken, natural, effortless Being-Consciousness that is compatible with all states. Equivalent to *Nirvana*.

Samadhi: A state of protracted engrossment or unbroken spiritual contemplation.

Samantabhadra: The primordial Buddha, a.k.a. *Adi-Buddha*, who is akin to *Siva* in tantric Saivism.

Samaya: A set of vows or precepts given to Tibetan Buddhist initiates.

Sambhogakaya: The Bliss, or Light, Body. The *Dharmakaya* as Blessing/Blissing Clear-Light Energy. Equivalent to Hindu *Shakti* and the Christian Holy Spirit/Ghost.

Samsara: A Sanskrit term that means "wandering." The cycle of death and rebirth, wherein individuals (*samsarins*) blindly meander from one conditioned state to another while failing to recognize and realize the timeless, unconditioned "State" (or non-state), *Nirvana*, that underlies and transcends all states.

Sat: Being.

Sat-Cit-Ananda: Being-Consciousness-Bliss.

Satsang: Fellowship with Being; Divine Communion.

Semde: The Mind Division (or Series), which is one of three scriptural divisions in Dzogchen: *Semde* (Mind), *Longde* (Space), and *Menngagde* (Secret or Instruction). *Semde* emphasizes the practice of presence; *Longde* focuses on empty space in relation to the Natural State; and *Menngagde* pertains to *trekcho* and *togal* teachings.

Shakti: Divine Power, or Clear-Light Energy. Equivalent to the Buddhist *Sambhogakaya* and the Christian Holy Spirit.

Shaktipat: The descent of Divine Power (or Grace), which can occur spontaneously in a disciple or be instigated by a spiritual master.

Siddha: A "Completed One." Equivalent to a Buddha.

Siddhi: Paranormal power possessed by a yogi or *Siddha*.

Siva: The personification of the Absolute in Hindu Shaivism. Akin to the *Adi-Buddha*, or *Samantabhadra*, in Vajrayana Buddhism.

Siva-Shakti: The Absolute (or Divine Being) depicted as Consciousness-Power rather than just Consciousness (*Siva*).

Sushumna: The Hindu yoga analogue for *avadhuti* (see *avadhuti*).

Sutra: "Thread" or scripture.

Svabhavakaya: The so-called Fourth Body, described as the union or non-separation of the three *Kayas* of the *Trikaya*. Because it just describes the unified State of the *Trikaya* after Enlightenment, it isn't a distinct Body per se.

Tantra: The term derives from "tan," which means to weave and expand. A *tantric* yogi weaves the strands of his nature into a unified whole, which frees and "expands" (or de-contracts) his consciousness. Spiritual alchemy: the transubstantiation of one's entire being into single, radiant Intensity.

Tathagata: A Buddha, or "thus-gone one," who unbrokenly and irreversibly abides in Thusness, or Suchness, or Beingness.

Tathagatagarbha: The "womb" or matrix where a Buddha, or "thus-gone one," is "reborn," or Awakened. Akin to the "cave of the Heart" in Hinduism.

Tathata: Thusness, Suchness, or Beingness. A synonym for *Dharmata*.

Terma: A "treasure teaching" buried or hidden by earlier masters and then later recovered.

Thigle: Luminous sphere or "drop" of rainbow light that is a manifestation of the Clear Light.

Togal: "Leap-Over" or "Direct Crossing." Directly contacting Spirit, the *Sambhogakaya*, or "Other Side," and contemplating/conducting its Clear-Light Energy. The "conductivity" aspect of *rigpa*, wherein the yogi experiences four progressive states, or "visions," of Enlightenment that culminate in the realization of *Dharmata*, the *Dharmakaya* as universal Suchness, or Beingness.

Trekcho: "Breakthrough." The aspect of *rigpa* that focuses on cutting (or breaking) through "spiritual materialism" (meaning all that is not Spirit) to get to Spirit, the *Sambhogakaya*, or "Other Side."

Trikaya: The Buddhist Triple Body (*Dharmakaya*, *Sambhogakaya*, *Nirmanakaya*). The *Dharmakaya* viewed three-dimensionally as transcendental, universal Consciousness, Blessing/Blissing Clear-Light Energy, and immanent, embodied Consciousness.

Upadesha: Teaching or instruction provided by a spiritual guru or preceptor.

Upaya: Skillful means.

Vajra Chain: Strings of connected *thigle* that, per standard *togal* teachings, comprise the objects of reality. The *Vajra chain* of Awareness can be construed as a synonym for the indestructible Light-Energy continuum of the *Dharmakaya*.

Vajrakaya: The "Indestructible Body" of full Enlightenment, meaning the post-Enlightenment *Sambhogakaya* realized as inseparable from the uncreated *Dharmakaya*.

Vajrayana: "Diamond Vehicle" tantric Buddhism, which seeks to "cut through" obstacles to Enlightenment by alchemically integrating and transcending them.

Vayus: The five *pranic* winds in Hindu yoga.

Vedanta: This term literally means "end of the Vedas." It is an umbrella term for the many sub-traditions, ranging from dualism to nondualism, that have a common connection to the Principal Upanishads, the Brahma Sutras, and the Bhagavad Gita.

Vijnana: This term has two meanings: 1) consciousness functioning as discriminating intelligence, the "higher mind," and 2) consciousness functioning dualistically, meaning at every level of mind.

Vijnamaya kosha: The sheath composed of understanding and discrimination. The "lower mind" coordinates sensory input and general mental activity, but understanding (*vijnana*) is a higher cognitive function. In *Vedanta*, the fourth of five sheaths covering the Self.

Yana: Vehicle, or way of crossing, to the "Other Shore," meaning *Nirvana*.

Yidam: A personal meditation deity; equivalent to *ishta-devata* in Hinduism.

Yogacara: The Mahayana Buddhist "Mind-Only" school, which consists of two distinct subschools: *Vijnaptimatra* (which asserts that all things are mere mental projections), and *Cittamatra* (which views all things as manifestations of universal Mind).

Zen: The term *Zen* (*Ch'an* in Chinese) derives from *dhyana* (Sanskrit), which means meditation. Hence, Zen Buddhism is Buddhism which emphasizes meditation while deemphasizing other aspects of *Buddhadharma*.

Spiritual Reading List

Advaita Vedanta

<u>Highly Recommended</u>

Ashtavakra Gita, trans. Hari Prasad Shastri. (Timeless Advaita Vedanta text. Available at www.shantisadan.org. Other translations also available.)

Be As You Are: The Teachings of Ramana Maharshi, David Godman. (Best introductory book on the teachings of Ramana Maharshi.)

Sat-Darshana Bhashya and Talks with Maharshi, Sri Ramanasramam. (A learned devotee's in-depth consideration of Ramana Maharshi's teachings within the framework of Indian-yogic philosophy.)

Sri Ramana Gita, Ramana Maharshi. (An utterly unique, ultra-profound text that details the function of the Amrita Nadi in the Self-realization process.)

Talks with Sri Ramana Maharshi, Ramana Maharshi. (Must-reading. A truly great and inspiring book. Avoid the dumbed-down version published by Inner Directions.)

(*Sat-Darshana Bhashya*, *Sri Ramana Gita*, and *Talks with Sri Ramana Maharshi* are available at www.arunachala.org.)

<u>Recommended</u>

Be Who You Are (or any of Jean Klein's books), Jean Klein.

I Am That: Talks with Sri Nisargadatta Maharaj, Maurice Frydman. (Classic, über-popular text.)

Silence of the Heart, Robert Adams.

Vivekachudamani (Crest Jewel of Discrimination), trans. Swami Prabhavananda and Christopher Isherwood. (Other translations of Shankara's teachings also available.)

Who Am I? Meditation, Ramaji. (If you like this text, get his *The Spiritual Heart*.)

Buddhism (Original)

Highly Recommended

Some Sayings of the Buddha: According to the Pali Canon, F.L. Woodward. (Easily the finest presentation of the Buddha's core teachings.)

The Wings to Awakening: An Anthology from the Pali Canon, Thanissaro Bhikku. (Outstanding translation of and commentary on the Buddha's essential meditation teachings. Free download available on the Internet.)

Recommended

Buddhism: An Outline of its Teachings and Schools, Hans Wolfgang Schuman. (Solid academic book.)

In the Buddha's Words: An Anthology of Discourses from the Pali Canon, Bhikku Bodhi. (Comprehensive introduction to the Buddha's teachings.)

Mindfulness in Plain English, Venerable Henepola Gunaratana. (Basic introductory text on insight meditation.)

The Doctrine of Awakening: The Attainment of Self-Mastery According to the Earliest Buddhist Texts, Julius Evola (Unique consideration of Pali Buddhism.)

The Heart of Buddhist Meditation, Nyaponika Thera. (Classic text on insight meditation.)

The Living Thoughts of Gotama the Buddha, Ananda Coomaraswamy and I. B. Horner. (Classic text. Excellent introduction to Buddhism.)

The Way of Non-Attachment, Dhiravamsa. (Unique Krishnamurti-influenced book on insight meditation. Out of print.)

Buddhism (Tibetan)

<u>Highly Recommended</u>

Principal Yogacara Texts: Indo-Tibetan Sources of Dzogchen Mahamudra, Rodney P. Devenish. (Easily the best Yogacara text I've encountered.)

Teachings of Tibetan Yoga, Garma C.C. Chang. (Superb Mahamudra presentation. Must-reading for serious meditators.)

The Cycle of Day and Night, Namkhai Norbu. (Outstanding Dzogchen meditation manual. Must-reading for serious meditators.)

The Golden Letters, John Myrdhin Reynolds. (Scholarly exposition of the history and practice of Dzogchen in relation to the Garab Dorje, the first teacher of Dzogchen.)

The Precious Treasury of the Way of Abiding, Longchen Rabjam. (Marvelous ultra-mystical text by a revered Vajrayana master. If you appreciate this book, get *A Treasure Trove of Scriptural Transmission: A Commentary on The Precious Treasury of the Basic Space of Phenomena*, by *the same author*. Other translations/annotations of Rabjam's texts are available.)

Recommended

Cutting Through Spiritual Materialism, Chogyam Trungpa. (Enlightening text by a modern "crazy wisdom" master.)

Naked Awareness, Karma Chagme. (Excellent material on Dzogchen and Mahamudra.)

Self-Liberation Though Seeing with Naked Awareness, John Myrdhin Reynolds. (Compare this translation of/commentary on Padmasambhava's *Yoga of Knowing the Mind and Seeing Reality* to W.Y. Evans-Wentz's in *The Tibetan Book of the Great Liberation*.)

The Supreme Source, Namkhai Norbu. (The fundamental tantric text of Dzogchen.)

The Tibetan Book of the Great Liberation, W.Y. Evans-Wentz. (Classic translation of/commentary on Padmasambhava's *Yoga of Knowing the Mind and Seeing Reality*. Compare this translation/commentary to John Myrdhin Reynolds's in *Self-Liberation Through Seeing with Naked Awareness*. Skip Carl Jung's ridiculous "Psychological Commentary.")

Tibetan Yoga and Secret Doctrines, W.Y. Evans-Wentz. (Classic, ultra-mystical text.)

Wonders of the Natural Mind, Tenzin Wangyal. (The essence of Dzogchen in the Native Bon Tradition of Tibet.)

(Although I have little good to say about Longchen Rabjam's *Precious Treasury of the Genuine Meaning*, it's must-reading for those interested in standard Dzogchen *togal*, as is Jigme Lingpa's *Yeshe Lama*, another text I hold in low regard. Sam van Schaik's *Approaching the*

Great Perfection: Simultaneous and Gradual Methods of Dzogchen Practice in the Longchen Nyingtig and *Naked Seeing: The Great Perfection, the Wheel of Time and Visionary Buddhism in Renaissance Tibet* by Christopher Hatchell are interesting, information-packed academic texts that serious students of *togal* will appreciate.)

Buddhism (Zen)

Highly Recommended

The Diamond Sutra and the Sutra of Hui Neng, trans. A.F. Price. (Other translations of these timeless sutras also available.)

Tracing Back the Radiance: Chinul's Korean Way of Zen, Robert Buswell, Jr. (Outstanding account of a great Zen master's spiritual evolution.)

The Zen Teaching of Huang Po, John Blofeld. (Easily the best book on Zen.)

Recommended

Kensho, The Heart of Zen, Thomas Cleary. (My favorite Cleary text on Zen.)

Practical Zen: Meditation and Beyond, Julian Daizan Skinner. (Excellent beginner-intermediate Zen instruction text.)

The Lankavatara Sutra, trans. D.T. Suzuki. (Avoid Red Pine's "butchered" translation.)

The Practice of Zen, Garma C.C. Chang. (Great autobiographical accounts of enlightenment. Out of print.)

The Rinzai Zen Way: A Guide to Practice, Meido Moore. (Excellent beginner-intermediate Zen instruction text.)

The Three Pillars of Zen, Philip Kapleau. (Classic, popular Rinzai Zen text that emphasizes the *satori* experience.)

The Way of Zen, Alan Watts. (Classic introductory text by the godfather of American Zen.)

Zen Mind, Beginner's Mind, Shunryu Suzuki. (Classic, ultra-popular Soto Zen text.)

Zen Teaching of Instantaneous Awakening, Ch'an Master Hui Hai; trans. John Blofeld. (Fine Dharma instructions by a great Chinese Ch'an master.)

(Scholarly types will enjoy Heinrich Dumoulin's *Zen Buddhism: A History (India and China)* and *Zen Buddhism: A History (Japan)*, Vol. 2. Serious students of Buddhist philosophy will appreciate Garma C.C. Chang's *The Buddhist Teaching of Totality*, which expounds Hwa Yen Buddhism's all-embracing philosophy in relation to Zen. If you enjoy reading Zen, check out Thomas Cleary's numerous books at Amazon.com. Edward Conze's *Selected Sayings from the Perfection of Wisdom* is a fine anthology of sayings from the Prajnaparamita Sutras, including the *Heart Sutra*.)

Christianity, Judaism, and Gnosticism

<u>Highly Recommended</u>

Meditations on the Tarot, Valentin Tomberg. (An astonishing journey into Christian Hermeticism. Must-reading for anyone interested in Christian mysticism.)

Meister Eckhart. (*The Complete Mystical Works of Meister Eckhart* is the book I recommend—but it costs $98. *Meister Eckhart*, trans. Raymond B. Blakney, is a fine compilation of Eckhart's sermons, and goes for about $15. Scholarly types will want to supplement either of the aforementioned books with *The Mystical Thought of Meister Eckhart* by Bernard McGinn.)

Mysticism, Evelyn Underwood. (Wonderful, classic, early twentieth-century text by the first lady of Christian mysticism.)

The Foundations of Mysticism. Bernard McGinn. (Extraordinary presentation of the Western mystical tradition. Must-reading for scholarly types.)

Recommended

Inner Christianity, Richard Smoley. (Clear and thoughtful guide to the esoteric Christian tradition.)

Jesus Christ, Sun of God, David Fideler (Fascinating read on ancient cosmology, gnostic symbolism, Pythagorean number theory, and Hellenistic gematria.)

Jewish Meditation, Aryeh Kaplan.

Open Mind, Open Heart, Thomas Keating. (Classic, best-selling text on the Gospel's contemplative dimension.)

The Big Book of Christian Mysticism: The Essential Guide to Contemplative Spirituality, Carl McColman. (Good introductory text and resource guide for those interested in Christian mysticism.)

The Mystic Christ, Ethan Walker. (Excellent book for Christians.)

The Practice of the Presence of God, Brother Lawrence, Robert Edmondson, and Jonathon Wilson-Hartgrove. (Classic text on the practice of establishing a conscious relationship with the Divine.)

The Secret Book of John, trans. Stevan Davies.

The Sermon on the Mount According to Vedanta, Swami Prabhavananda.

The Way of a Pilgrim and the Pilgrim Continues His Way, Multiple fine translations available. (Inspiring book for practitioners of prayer and mantra meditation.)

(Scholarly types into Western Christian mysticism will love all the fine texts by Prof. Bernard McGinn. Check out his seven-volume *The Presence of God Series*, which, begins with the highly recommended *The Foundations of Mysticism*. Beyond this series, McGinn has graced us with *The Essential Writings of Christian Mysticism*, an immensely rich anthology of the greatest Christian mystical literature. Selections in this volume include writings from such great mystics as Origen, Augustine, Pseudo-Dionysius the Areopagite, St. John of the Cross, Bernard of Clairvaux, Meister Eckhart, John Ruysbroeck, and many more. For a scholarly consideration of Jewish mysticism, I recommend Gershom Scholem's *Major Trends in Jewish Mysticism and* Moshe Idel's *Kabbalah: New Perspectives*. Scholem's text is the canonical modern work on the nature and history of Jewish mysticism, while Idel's is the foremost scholarly consideration of Kabbalah.)

Daism

<u>Highly Recommended</u>

Hridaya Rosary (Four Thorns of Heart-Instruction), Adi Da Samraj. (Excellent technical devotional-meditation book.)

The Knee of Listening, Adi Da Samraj. (Best spiritual autobiography ever written. Must-reading for mystics. Get a copy of the latest edition, but also get a copy of an earlier edition written under either the names of Franklin Jones or Bubba Free John. These earlier editions, unlike later and current editions, contain Da's outstanding

"Meditation of Understanding," instructions on the practice of "real meditation," or "radical understanding.")

The Liberator: The "Radical" Reality-Teachings of The Great Avataric Sage, Adi Da Samraj. Adi Da Samraj.

The Method of the Siddhas, Adi Da Samraj. (A truly great spiritual book. Out of print and only available used. Try to get a copy written under the names of either Franklin Jones or Bubba Free John. The current revised edition of the book, entitled *My "Bright" Word*, lacks the direct visceral impact of the original text.)

The Pneumaton, Adi Da Samraj. (Ultra-esoteric consideration of "Pneuma," the Spirit.)

The Way of Perfect Knowledge: The "Radical" Practice of Transcendental Spirituality in the Way of Adidam, Adi Da Samraj.

Recommended

He-And-She Is Me: The Indivisibility of Consciousness and Light In the Divine Body of the Ruchira Avatar, Adi Da Samraj.

Ruchira Avatara Hridaya-Siddha Yoga: The Divine (and Not Merely Cosmic) Spiritual Baptism in the Way of Adidam, Adi Da Samraj.

Santosha Adidam: The Essential Summary of the Divine Way of Adidam, Adi Da Samraj.

The All-Completing and Final Divine Revelation to Mankind: A Summary Description Of The Supreme Yoga Of The Seventh Stage Of Life In The Divine Way Of Adidam, Adi Da Samraj.

(The four books on the Recommended List contain a number of the same essays. Nonetheless, each book includes enough unique material to merit its reading.)

Hinduism (Yoga)

Highly Recommended

The Bhagavad Gita, translations by Eknath Easwaran, Swami Prabhavananda and Christopher Isherwood, S. Radhakrishnan. (Many other fine translations/annotations also available.)

The Yoga of Spiritual Devotion: A Modern Translation of the Narada Bhakti Sutras, Prem Prakesh. (A simple, inspiring text on the spiritual path of love and devotion.)

The Yoga Sutras of Patanjali, Edwin F. Bryant. (A 600-page tome that provides a wealth of information on the history, philosophy, and practice of classical yoga. Serious students of yoga will want to read this text as well as Swami Hariharananda Aranya's *Yoga Philosophy of Patanjali*.)

Yoga Philosophy of Patanjali, Swami Hariharananda Aranya. (A unique and profound account of classical yoga by a scholar-monk.)

Recommended

Be Here Now, Baba Ram Dass. (Classic introductory book on Eastern philosophy. An easy and entertaining read.)

How to Know God, Prabhavananda and Isherwood. (Best introduction to the yoga philosophy of Patanjali.)

The Essential Swami Ramdas, Swami Ramdas. (Inspiring writings of a great twentieth-century *bhakti* yogi.)

The Gospel of Sri Ramakrishna, Swami Nikhilananda. (A revered *bhakti* classic.)

The Synthesis of Yoga, Sri Aurobindo. (Profound essays on yoga by Sri

Aurobindo, the renowned twentieth-century Indian guru-philosopher. If you appreciate this book and crave more Aurobindo, get a copy of *The Life Divine*.)

The Upanishads, translations by Mascara, and by Prabhavananda and Isherwood. (Other fine translations also available.)

The Yoga Tradition, Georg Feuerstein. (Outstanding reference book on the history, literature, philosophy, and practice of yoga.)

Kashmir Shaivism

<u>Highly Recommended</u>

Pratyabhijnahrdayam: The Secret of Self-Recognition, Jaideva Singh. (The basic introductory handbook to the abstruse philosophical system of recognition. Not for the intellectually challenged. *The Doctrine of Recognition*, out of print but available as an ebook, is, thanks to the editing of Paul Muller-Ortega, the best version of this text.)

Siva Sutras: The Yoga of Supreme Identity, Jaideva Singh. (The foundational text of Kashmir Shaivism.)

The Doctrine of Vibration, Mark S.G. Dyczkowski. (A scholarly analysis of the doctrines and practices of Kashmir Shaivism.)

The Philosophy of Sadhana, Deba Brata SenSharma. (Outstanding text that deals clearly and extensively with the ultra-important topic of *Shaktipat*, the Descent of Divine Power, or Grace. Must-reading for serious mystics.)

The Triadic Heart of Siva, Paul Eduardo Muller-Ortega. (An ultra-esoteric text about the Heart (*Hridaya*) as Ultimate Reality, Emissional Power, and Embodied Cosmos.)

Recommended

Kundalini, The Energy of the Depths, Lilian Silburn. (As an Amazon.com reviewer puts it, "The foremost modern exposition of Kundalini.")

Spanda Karikas: The Divine Creative Pulsation, Jaideva Singh. (An elaboration of the dynamic aspect of Transcendental Consciousness.)

Miscellaneous

Highly Recommended

The First and Last Freedom, J. Krishnamurti. (Must-reading for all mystics. If you appreciate this book and want to read more Krishnamurti, get his multivolume *Commentaries on Living*.)

Introduction to Objectivist Epistemology, Ayn Rand. (Must-reading for all mystics.)

Objectivism: The Philosophy of Ayn Rand, Leonard Peikoff. (Must-reading for all mystics.)

The Way of Chuang Tzu, Thomas Merton. (Other translations also available.)

Recommended

A Brief History of Everything, Ken Wilber. (If you're interested in "integral thinking," you'll enjoy this book. If you appreciate it, get *Sex, Ecology, Spirituality: The Spirit of Evolution*.)

Alan Oken's Complete Astrology, Alan Oken. (Best overall book on astrology.)

Ayurveda: The Science of Self-Healing, Vasant Lad. (Fascinating and enlightening exposition of the principles and practical applications of Indian Ayurveda, the oldest healing system in the world.)

Awaken Healing Energy Through the Tao, Mantak Chia. (Classic introductory handbook to the practice and principles of Taoist energy yoga.)

The Mystique of Enlightenment: The Radical Ideas of U.G. Krishnamurti, U.G. Krishnmurti (U.G. was the ultimate spiritual iconoclast. Jean Klein called him "pathological." I call him "a great read.")

The Perennial Philosophy, Aldous Huxley. (Classic text by a great writer.)

The Tao Te Ching. (Numerous translations available.)

www.ingramcontent.com/pod-product-compliance
Lightning Source LLC
LaVergne TN
LVHW051600070426
835507LV00021B/2689